By the Goodness of God

By the Goodness of God

An Autobiography

John G. Innis

Abingdon Press
Nashville

BY THE GOODNESS OF GOD: AN AUTOBIOGRAPHY

This book is printed on acid-free paper.

Library of Congress Cataloging-in-Publication Data

Innis, John G., 1948-
By the goodness of God : an autobiography / John G. Innis.
p. cm.
ISBN 0-687-02238-X (adhesive binding : alk. paper)
1. Innis, John G., 1948- 2. United Methodist Church in Liberia—Bishops—Biography. I. Title.
BX8495.I69 A3 2003
287'.6'092—dc21

2003011633

03 04 05 06 07 08 09 10 11 12 – 10 9 8 7 6 5 4 3 2 1

MANUFACTURED IN THE UNITED STATES OF AMERICA

Contents

Guide to Acronyms

Main Players in Liberia and/or the Liberian Civil War

AFL Armed Forces of Liberia. The name for government troops during the last part of the 20th century.

ECOMOG West African Peace Keeping Force. Troops sent by the Economic Community of West African States (ECOWAS) to try and maintain peace during the civil war in the 1990s.

IGNU Interim Government of National Unity. One of the governments organized during the civil war.

INPFL Independent National Patriotic Front of Liberia. A rebel group led by Prince Y. Johnson, and a rival group to the NPFL led by Charles Taylor. It was responsible for killing President Doe in 1990.

LFF Liberia Frontier Force. Early twentieth century government army troops.

LNGB Liberia National Guard Brigade. Another incarnation of the Liberian army.

LNTG-II Liberia National Transitional Government. Another attempt by the Economic Community of West African States to create political stability in the country in the 1990s.

NPFL National Patriotic Front of Liberia. Rebel group led by Charles Taylor.

PRC People's Redemption Council, the military junta, headed by Samuel Doe, that replaced the Tolbert government after the 1980 coup.

ULIMO United Liberation Movement for Democracy in Liberia. Originally organized to fight the NPFL, made up mostly of members of the Krahn group who were loyal to Samuel Doe, the leader of the rebel group that assassinated President Tolbert in 1980.

ULIMO-J A faction of the ULIMO, led by General Roosevelt Johnson.

ULIMO-K Another faction of the ULIMO, led by General Albert Kromah.

Other Acronyms

AME African Methodist Episcopal Church.

ASAP All Students Alliance Party, a leading student group at University of Liberia in the 1970s.

BBC British Broadcasting Company.

CEF Christian Education Foundation of Liberia, founded by the Reverand Abba Karnga.

CEM Christian Extension Ministries, based in Buchanan.

ELBC Radio station of the Liberian Broadcasting Corporation, Monrovia.

ELWA Christian radio station in Monrovia: "Eternal Love Winning Africa." Seized by Charles Taylor's forces in the early 1990s and turned into a government propaganda station.

GBGM General Board of Global Ministries (of The United Methodist Church).

LAC Liberia Annual Conference (of The United Methodist Church).

LAMCO Iron ore mining company, a joint venture of Liberian government with American and Swedish investors.

LPA Legal power of attorney arrangement made with merchants and businessmen.

SDA Seventh Day Adventist.

SUP Student Unification Party, campus group at University of Liberia in the 1970s.

UMC The United Methodist Church.

UMCOR United Methodist Committee on Relief.

UMYF United Methodist Youth Fellowship.

UMW United Methodist Women.

VOA Voice of America.

YFC Youth for Christ. Organization started in the 1940s in the U.S. to evangelize high school students.

Acknowledgments

I must first give God the glory for this book, because it is all about God's goodness to me. The book may tell the story of my life, but without God's care and loving-kindness shown to me, the story might not have been told and not told in this literary form. God has not only sustained my life and prepared me to undertake this venture, but God has also helped make this narrative a reality through the contributions of many wonderful, caring, and generous people—many of whom have now gone to rest with the Lord.

The Liberia Annual Conference of The United Methodist Church has given me tremendous financial, moral, spiritual, and academic support and I am immensely grateful, particularly to the former resident bishops, the Reverend Dr. Bennie D. Warner and the Reverend Dr. Arthur F. Kulah. The UMC's General Board of Global Ministries also played a helpful and inspiring role in the writing of this book, with special thanks to Dr. Randolph Nugent, Dr. Kenneth Lugent, and Dr. Paul Dirdak. Many thanks also to my wonderful colleagues at the Board and at Sager-Brown Center in Baldwin, Louisiana. All of you touched my life in marvelous ways.

I also want to give special thanks to my pastor, the Reverend Richard Whitefleet-Smith of the Quinsigamond United Methodist Church in Worcester, Massachusetts, who provided much useful editorial advice. So, too, did the Reverend Dr. Nathan Junius and the Reverend Dr. G. Solomon Gueh, and I thank them also. They encouraged me to undertake this project because they felt it was worth the effort.

The former students, teachers, and staff of the Camphor United Methodist Mission School in Grand Bassa County, Liberia, inspired and motivated me in various ways during my working, teaching, and learning experiences at Camphor, and so played a unique role in helping to make this book possible.

I am very grateful to the office staff of the Liberia Annual Conference Secretariat who made available to me the conference journals, enabling me to obtain vital information. To Coordinator Joel Gould, who personally provided useful information which helped in reconstructing the story of my life, I give my special thanks. Other helpful staff were Titi Blamo and Andrew Nimely.

Several people made up a small but efficient work team, both assisting in the preparation of the manuscript and taking care of other matters so that I had time to write. To Zehyu Wuduorgar I owe an immense dept of gratitude for his wise editorial counsel, his hard work, and his untiring commitment to this project. Zehyu and I spent sleepless weeks and months dictating, writing, and editing the manuscript.

Judith Dean-Walker, my office asssitant who ran the office very ably during my absence, is another dedicated teammate of this special project. I very much appreciate the tireless hours she spent at the computer typing out not only the handwritten script but also typing and retyping the several edited versions. And while Judith was on maternity leave, I was most grateful to her brother, Joel Dean, who spent a number of weeks continuing the typing.

To the rest of my office staff I extend a hearty thank-you. Archie Kiawu was the chauffeur who drove us safely to and from work as well as other places we needed to go. J. Toe Blamoh was the liaison officer who took care of our visitors and other office-related matters. Nathan Allison took care of the janitorial aspect of the office. Thank you all.

It would take more space and words than we have room for to express my love and gratitude to my family for their help and for the sacrifices they made so that this work could get done. I am so very grateful to my darling wife, Irene, for her vital contribution to the book. She was able to provide most of the information that I couldn't readily recall. In the midst of her heavy domestic and academic schedule, she also provided editorial assistance. I thank her and our children, Chenda, Janjay, Blason, and Bleejay for their love, understanding, patience, and encouragement. My frequent travels away from home robbed them of the time we should have spent together as a family. And then when I was at home, much of my time was spent at the computer. The rest of the children, Youjay, Trocon, Garmonyu, and Genca, were not always available when I started this project. But I regularly contacted them in Ghana where they were living as refugees as a result of the horrific seven-year civil war in Liberia. They, too, approved of the book and also supplied helpful information.

I have not named other persons and institutions who contributed to the successful completion of this project, not out of ingratitude but rather because of my inability to recall their names. Please forgive me if you do not find your name here, but know that I extend my grateful thanks.

May God bless all of us for what we have been able to achieve together—the publication of this book.

Introduction

In *By the Goodness of God* I attempt to portray my life from birth to the present time. I use the word *attempt* because of my long-standing reluctance to write a book of this nature. There are several reasons for this reluctance. First, I have never considered myself a gifted writer. Nor did I ever dream of undertaking such an important literary exercise. Second, although I was a student of history, I had never worked on any historical project that would provide a guide for a book such as this that covers a fifty-year span and deals with so many events, dates, and the many institutions and people who have touched my life. The only previous documentary I had put together was a brief history of Camphor Mission, the school where I taught for many years, which we used as an information handout. And third, if it were published, would anyone read it?

Why, then, did I change my mind? God has been my ultimate source of inspiration. God's goodness to me from my birth onward gave me the sense of purpose and courage to finally tell the story of my life. God also worked through The United Methodist Church, and through friends, through personal contacts. Their appreciation and encouragement helped remove the barriers in my mind. The following story is an example of those through whom God spoke to make this publication a reality.

In December 1998 I was on a plane traveling from New York to Louisiana. Seated next to me was an elderly woman. When I greeted her after takeoff, she said, "Your accent tells me that you are not from here."

"No, I'm not," I responded. "I'm from Liberia in West Africa."

"But how did you come to the States?" she asked.

"Well, I'm a United Methodist minister," I told her. "I was employed in 1996 by the General Board of Global Ministries of The United Methodist Church, headquartered in New York."

"Do you have a family? Where are they?"

"In Baldwin, Louisiana," I told her.

"You must be happy they're with you," she said.

"I certainly am!" I responded.

Deeply touched by the lady's friendly concern, I decided to share some of my personal experiences with her, especially the rough times I passed through during the terrible civil war in Liberia, and how God protected me and saved my life.

"I'm alive today," I told her, "not because of any goodness in me, but rather as the result of the gracious, caring, and loving ways of God for me. I was beaten, shot at, bruised, and cut on the head by rebel soldiers who forcibly occupied the United Methodist mission school that I administered before and during the early years of the war. If it had not been for God's divine intervention, I would have died—and never seen my wife and children, or my relatives and friends again."

To my surprise, my seatmate responded by saying, "God will continue to bless you." And then she added, "God created you for a purpose, and you will see in the not-too-distant future what God has for you."

The unforgettable memory of my brief encounter with this kind and perceptive lady shows how God inspired me, even through strangers, to develop the willpower to attempt this book. I am most grateful to Almighty God, who was my primary source of inspiration and courage, and who moved people to challenge, inspire, and motivate me to write. Like the apostle Paul, I, too, can now testify that "I can do all things through Christ who strengthens me."

In the book I describe my life growing up in rural Whayongar Town in Grand Bassa County, under the loving care of my maternal grandparents. I share a little about what it was like to be part of a close-knit village, and describe some of our childhood games. The next chapters describe the abrupt changes in my life demanded by my father, first to boarding school, and then to the big city of Monrovia where I was supposed to go to school but became essentially a somewhat abused houseboy for a distant relative, eventually a street boy, and briefly a member of a street gang. When I finally got back to my father, though he was sure I would never be educated, he did enter me again in the mission boarding school, Camphor. Determined to prove that I would be educated, I completed the first six grades in four years.

The next chapters cover my time in high school in our county capital, a stint of teaching back in Camphor to earn money for college, then university in Monrovia, and coming back to Camphor as principal of the school. The story of how I met and married my beautiful wife and how our union has been blessed has its own chapter, as does our three-year period of study in the United States at Saint Paul School of Theology in Kansas City, Missouri.

Returning to Liberia, we had a brief two years of relatively peaceful time at Camphor before the outbreak of war. The bloody and destructive Liberian Civil War takes up four chapters as I try to give a brief picture of the trauma and horrors of this conflict that has been called a senseless war. During this time we tried to keep Camphor school going, even after the campus was destroyed.

When the General Board of Global Ministries asked me to work with UMCOR, my family and I moved to the United States. During that time, my name was put on the list to be considered for the position of bishop of Liberia. The story of how I became bishop occupies a whole chapter.

Before I end the book, I have a chapter dedicated to my brothers and sisters and the complementary role we have played in one anothers' lives. A final chapter acknowledges the tremendous blessings God has given me through The United Methodist Church—blessings I could not see for much of my life. In the Epilogue, I reaffirm my faith in the Lord Jesus Christ and my commitment to servanthood in God, through the Church, to humanity.

To God be the glory for the great things God has done for me.

Chapter One

A Happy Childhood in Whayongar Town

September 16, 1948, was a day of great rejoicing in rural Whayongar Town, Grand Bassa, Liberia. A boy was born to a daughter of the town, Conwree Neor Innis, and Philip Innis. His parents named him John.

"This boy will be our future liberator," the people said. "He will save us from the injustice and cruelty of soldiers and government officials, from forced labor, oppressive taxes, and terrible punishments."

In later years I looked back at this prophetic expectation as a kind of signpost for my life. But while I was growing up in Whayongar Town, for the most part I took the attitude of the people for granted, just as I did my playmates' always choosing me as their leader. But at one point I did ask my maternal grandparents, with whom I lived, why I was singled out in the thinking of the townspeople. I was not the only boy child born in 1948 in Whayogar Town, my mother's hometown. "It's because your father was educated by Western standards," they told me. "Therefore you, too, will be educated. You will become a leader in the Liberian government and will free us from government oppression."

For many years before I was born, the people of Whayongar Town, as well as those of other rural areas of Liberia, were subjected to dehumanizing treatment both by soldiers of the Liberian Frontier Force (LFF) and by local government officials. One of the most feared forms of torture came during the collecting of "Head" and "Hut" taxes. The Liberian government not only imposed a tax on every rural hut or dwelling in every community, but they also taxed every family head. The vast majority of rural people were very poor and couldn't afford to pay these taxes. So revenue collectors and the LFF soldiers who accompanied them devised special punishments for delinquents. One was to have the individual kneel on sharp broken palm kernel shells. Another was to make the person lie on his or her back with eyes open to the sun.

Kpee-kpee was another painful form of punishment. An ingenious foot cuff was made from two sticks twisted and tied at both ends around the calf of the leg. The rope at one end was tied tight while the other end was loose. The loosened portion was gradually tightened if the delinquent person delayed in paying the tax. Further delays caused further tightening, increasing the pain on the fibula. This would go on until someone volunteered to pay the tax. Sometimes the victim would have to pawn valuable possessions—sometimes even a daughter!

Rural people were forced to clear, plant, and harvest the farms of local government officials, district commissioners, clan, and paramount chiefs. They were also impelled by soldiers and officials to carry heavy loads on their heads and shoulders. These often consisted of chickens, goats, rice, and other provisions that had been forcibly collected from the people. At other times they had to carry the "official hammock." Since there were no motor roads through the rural areas in those days, traveling government officials were conveyed from one place to another in a hammock carried on the heads and shoulders of men from the rural villages. When public roads were constructed, it was through forced labor by workers using homemade machetes, hoes, and axes. No wonder the people of Whayongar Town were ready for a liberator.

Whayongar Town is located in Neepu Clan, District #4, in the coastal county of Grand Bassa in the West African State of Liberia. Bassa is the anglicized name for *Bahsor,* an ethnic group. Though the Bahsor, or *Bahsor-nyon,* according to the national census, form the second largest tribe in Liberia next to the Kpelle,[1] they occupy more than four political subdivisions or counties, while the Kpelles are mainly concentrated in one county.

My father, Philip Dwah Innis, came from Morblee, in Harlandsville Township, District #3, in Grand Bassa County. His parents were Gboryrun Dwah and his wife, Chenda. Grandpa Dwah had thirteen children: six boys—Miller, Zayway, Sunday, Alfred, Jeremiah, and Philip, my father; and seven girls—Blohso, Sarday, Julia, Yonnonkplen, Titi, Yarnein, and Kpayehwheh.

Grandpa Dwah sent my father when he was very young to live with the Reverend Joseph T. Innis in Upper Buchanan, a suburb of the capital of Grand Bassa County on the west Atlantic coast. In Liberia in those days, it was a common practice, termed the Ward System (WS), for indigenous families to send their children, mainly boys, to live with a settler family who were descendants of freed slaves from the United States that established modern Liberia. The first settlers came in the 1820s, and Liberia gained independence in 1847, but African Americans continued to emigrate through the rest of the nineteenth and into the twentieth centuries. In Liberian history they are referred to as Americo-Liberians. The boys often adopted the surname of the settler family, as my father did.

The original intent of the WS was "to educate, Christianize, and civilize" young Liberians based on Western standards. The Americo-Liberians were joined later in the nineteenth century by some people of color from the West Indies. Later emancipated Africans from the Congo basin joined them. These three groups constitute the settler class in Liberia, making up all told about 5 to 6 percent of the population.

Joseph Innis, Dad's guardian, was a Methodist pastor. He later became superintendent of Grand Bassa County, a political appointment. Hence my father was well placed to begin his Christian and his academic life. He started school in Upper Buchanan, the capital of Grand Bassa County, where some of his fellow students were prominent Liberians Arthur Summerville, Philip Brumskine, Hannibal Brumskine, and Samuel T. Summerville. Later Dad enrolled in Hazel Academy, where he finished the eighth grade before returning to Morblee. Hazel Academy was a Methodist institution until it was transformed into a public school and renamed Bassa High. Eventually he became a schoolteacher.

My father joined the Methodist Episcopal Church, now The United Methodist Church, in the latter part of 1930, and on his return to Morblee he became very active in the church. One of his early positions was that of choir director for Camphor Memorial Methodist Church, now Garfield Methodist Church in Tubmanville Township, Grand Bassa County. Later he became secretary of the St. John River District, MC and held this position for thirty-three years. He was much loved for his efficient and dedicated service.

Although he was a Christian, my father was a polygamist and had fourteen children. The five girls are Juah, the oldest of all of us, Sundaymah, Esther, Sayyea (whose nickname is Yeadoe) and Felicia (whose nickname is Tupee). The nine boys are James, Nathaniel, Roosevelt, Jerry, Dwahyuway, William, Patrick, Teedoe and myself—John.

My mother, Conwree, was also a devoted Christian and the mother of three children—Nathaniel, Felicia, and myself. I am the oldest. Mom was born in her home community of Whayongar Town, one of six children of Glor Neor and his wife, Kamah. Her three brothers are: Big Borbor, Small Borbor, and Levi; her two sisters are: Sorday and Posseh.

Mom first joined St. John Methodist Church in Neepu, her native clan. When she and Dad got married, she became a member of Camphor Memorial MC, where she sang in the choir and later served as a class leader. A committed Christian, she exhibited great love and care, not only for her own children and immediate relatives, but also for others outside the family circle.

Shortly after my birth, my mother left me with her parents, Glor Neor and Kamah, and returned to Morblee, my father's hometown. Though this action might seem to contradict my description of my mother's love and care, such is not the case. Her leaving me with her parents was simply a fulfillment of a prevailing cultural practice. It was common for grandparents to take care of their grandchildren, especially in the case of a first-born. The reason behind this practice still exists today among both rural and urban Liberians. Our people believe that a young woman giving birth for the first time is not experienced enough to take proper care of the baby. Since I was my mother's first child, my "grands" took me from her.

I found a cozy place in my grandparents' hearts. Since I was the only baby in the home, I was accorded all the necessary attention. I never went hungry, and whenever they suspected any sign of illness they took precautionary measures, using appropriate herbs. If the illness was beyond their control they would immediately inform my mother and father.

I grew up with my Aunt Posseh and my two cousins, Yonnin and Yarwhor, who were older than I. Aunt Posseh always teased me by saying, "Your grandparents will spoil you." I would go crying to my grands and repeat Aunt Posseh's statement. They would scold Aunt Posseh and warn her against making me feel dejected. But Aunt Posseh's teasing remarks were not meant to hurt. In reality, she complemented the love and care of my grandparents. Regrettably, Aunt Posseh died during the Liberian civil war.

Two of her daughters, Titi and Theresa, became very close to my family before her death. Titi died just four years after her mother.

I had many happy moments as a child growing up in Whayongar Town. All of us children enjoyed drawing images on the ground with our fingers or bamboo chips or small sticks. We would make tiny houses and villages out of moist sandy soil, bamboo twigs, leaves, and sticks, using both our hands and our feet. The dirt houses took the least time but were the most difficult to construct. We'd pile moist soil over a foot and ankle, patting the soil down with our hands, until it seemed firm enough. Then the foot would be gradually and delicately pulled away. If the soil had been sufficiently moist, evenly distributed, and properly molded on the foot, the house stood firm. Otherwise it collapsed. The hollow made by the foot produced a one-room house with an arch entrance. We'd construct several "foot" houses together to make a town or village, sometimes enclosing them with walls made of moist soil or bamboo twigs.

Like all children, we played athletic games, racing each other to determine who was the fastest. But some of our favorite games were word games. One was the leg-counting chant known as *Bloo Bloo*. The leader of the game kneels or squats in front of the others who sit close together with their legs stretched out in front of them. He gently brushes his fingertips over the thighs of each child in turn, chanting, *"Bloo, bloo."*

"Yaa, yaa," they respond in time with his chanting.

When he stops chanting, he asks the child whose leg he is touching, *"Nyen kin bho mza-ayeh?"* Meaning, "Whose leg do you wish to take out?"

"Mza-aye mbaa bho," the child might say. "I want to take out my daddy's leg."

The chanting and selection goes on until all the children's "legs," as well as the "legs" of their parents and family members, have been "taken out." No one can be named twice. (The full chant is given in appendix 1.)

Other songs and chants taught us to recognize wild birds and animals by their sounds and calls, which we learned to interpret and to imitate. The yellow rice bird, *nyanmana,* is believed to tease farmers before and after devouring the crop, calling *booga, booga*—the name of the most popular strain of locally cultivated rice! The chant we learned started with that mocking:

Booga, booga
Young nectar's sweet, sweet;
The owner's heart p-a-i-n-s;
Only my heart e-a-s-e-s.

We also had a sad song about the dove, one that not only tries to imitate its mournful coo, as you can hear when you sound out the words, but also refers to the rules of group eating. The rules for children decree that each child takes food from the bowl in turn, starting with the eldest and ending with the youngest. No one is allowed to take an extra large helping—that is a sign of greediness. Any child who tries to take more is scolded, beaten, or stopped from eating, as happened to the poor dove.

Sauhn plin-aye, Doo plin-aye:
Mouhn munye plin nyehn,
Noo nyan-mahn-in gbagbor du koo, koo, koo!
Ai say-o mdi poo-poo jayn
Mouhn da-o-wheah mu say, say, say.

Sauhn took his turn, Doo took his turn,
When I tried to take my turn,
With the butt of the cooking hook
Mother knocked my head bong, bong, bong!
If it weren't for my relation, brown pigeon,
For the highlands I'd have left long ago, ago, ago!

We had several songs that imitated the brown pigeon and also referred to the farming of rice and the need to protect the rice and crops at all stages from the birds. In the most popular version, the pigeon asks the farmer and his family in the first line, "Why do you go to the farm so early, before the day breaks?" The fact is that rice farmers leave town for their farms very early in the morning, since the farms are a good distance away and they want to drive away the birds that come in the early morning hours to feed on the seeds and grains.

In the second line of the song, the pigeon tells the farmer, "A lump of *Gbehzohn* [Grand Bassa] *dumboy* costs two cents." *Gbehzohn* is the original name of Grand Bassa County, and *dumboy* is the Bassa favorite dish. The farmer and his family shouldn't work so hard to keep the birds from eating the crops when they can eat their favorite food so cheaply! (See appendix 1 for this chant, and another one about the brown pigeon.)

Storytelling was a favorite evening event in Whayongar Town that all of us children eagerly looked forward to. After the evening meal, we would gather in the town's central courtyard under the silvery glow of the moon, or around the warm yellow flames of a kitchen hearth to hear the older folks tell us beautiful stories, and sometimes to tell them ourselves. Most of the stories featured *Sahn* as the main character. *Sahn,* Spider, is the symbol of gluttony, craftiness, selfishness, covetousness, slothfulness, and the like. Because of these negative qualities, he is popularly referred to as *Juku Sahn* or *Geekpeh Kadeaye.* The stories often showed us how Spider got his comeuppance. For one famous Spider story, see appendix 1.

Other popular stories featured *Deh Vennehn,* Big Monster, and *Ghee Vennehn,* Big Lord. Some were puzzle stories—*Dweyn Nouhn*—while others were epic tales, referred to as *Yuduahnkayu,* meaning "never-ending," featuring the legendary twin brothers, Zahntohn and Yukpeegar.

The simplest story was about Great, Great Big-Headed Tadpole—*Borhnor Du Gua Gua Gohno,* and was usually sung. For this and almost every story the narrator begins by saying, or singing, "I am present"—*"Mohn niowo."* The audience responds by singing the title refrain, *"Gohrhnor due gua gua gohno,"* "Great, Great Big-Headed Tadpole." As the story goes on in short phrases and clauses, the audience periodically repeats the refrain.

In the Bassa culture, every story begins with the narrator's placing himself or herself in the action of the story, "I am present." Sometimes the narrator would compare the height or age or mannerisms of a character with someone in the audience or in the village. The stories generally portrayed the struggle between good and evil, virtue and vice, love and hate, and both good and bad were the focal points. In concluding the story, the narrator would emphasize the good and the bad results, leaving it up to us children to decide which side to choose. Quite often, the good morals were the most appealing. But strangely, some kids wished they were Spider, so that they could eat as much food as he did, especially in those stories featuring Spider as a glutton.

Another game we children often played was holding church, and my friends selected me to pastor this mock church. As "pastor," I imitated the mannerisms and preaching style of the Reverend Alfred W. Page, who was then the pastor of St. John's Methodist Church in Neepu, where I was born and brought up, since he was the only spiritual leader I knew. This was not the only time I was chosen by my friends to be their leader.

Our time as children was not spent solely on fun and leisure. Every child in Whayongar Town had to help with the household work. We also helped our parents and grandparents on the farm and in the fields. Our main farm job was to help drive away the devouring rice birds. This was done at three different times in the growing season. The first was during planting time. The second came when the rice heads burst forth from the shoots and the flat husks began to swell with sweet milky nectar. The third was when the crop was ready to be harvested.

Children also helped in various community activities. House daubing was one of these. When a new house, created of poles and sticks, was ready to be daubed—plastered with clay—the owner would ask parents and grandparents to let their children help. The girls were assigned to work in the kitchen with the women preparing the food for the *Beewhor*—the daubing feast. The girls also helped the women haul water for the preparation of the mortar.

The boys helped with creating, carrying, and applying the mortar. The mortar was made of brown clay mixed with water and kneaded to the correct consistency. The older boys helped the men knead the mortar with their feet. The clay was taken either directly from the earth or from brown, abandoned termite hills. The little boys helped by carrying the mortar to the daubers, either on their heads or on their arms folded across their chests. The boy carrying the biggest lump of mortar was considered the strongest. The fastest hauler was rated the most hardworking. Of course we also tested our marksmanship by aiming small bits of mortar at each other!

Our childhood life in Whayongar Town did not always consist of fun and leisure. There were moments of misunderstanding, which often led to harsh exchanges of words, to fights, or to abrupt terminations of friendship, and sometimes to the formation of cliques. But these disruptions were only temporary, sometimes lasting for less than five or ten minutes. We usually made amends or simply forgot the incident and once more continued our routine activities. The older folk also helped to make peace among us, usually with the one word, *sorry*, spoken to console the aggrieved party. Then everything was over.

I am happy that the older folk of our village taught us the concept of peacemaking in times of conflict. It has paid off well in my life.

Note

1. There are more than twenty ethnic groups in Liberia, each with its own language.

Chapter Two

Two Weeks in My Father's Custody

When I was eight years old my parents divorced and my life changed drastically. Gboryun Dwah, my paternal grandfather, who represented Dad in the divorce proceedings, took me away from my maternal grandparents, who had nurtured, loved, and cherished me so dearly over the years. My father was determined that I would start my education.

When I learned that I would have to leave Whayongar Town with Grandfather Dwah, I wept bitterly. I was being taken away from my haven of boundless love, affection, and childhood security with my loving grandparents. I would no longer be with Aunt Pooseh and my cousins Yonnin and Yarwhor. I would no longer enjoy fun and games with my friends, or experience the high esteem in which the people of the town held me.

For Grandfather Dwah, my weeping was only a formality. The decision to take me away could not be reversed. Since I was too young to resist, I gave up the protest. I could have run away and hid until Grandfather Dwah left, but two additional factors helped me come to terms with the decision. The first had to do with my education. I knew that the people of Whayongar Town referred to me as their *kwee,* their educated one. Though that did not seem a meaningful challenge then, I felt somehow consoled by the thought of their expectation of me. And, more important, my grandparents, as well as the people of Whayongar Town, knew that my father had acquired a minimum Western education. They were eager for me also to get this kind of education.

Since I was going to live with my father, they did not show any signs of disapproval. Instead, they saw it as the beginning of their dream for my life.

The second consolation was Grandma Kamah. Just before Grandpa Dwah and I were going to leave, she called me aside and blessed me. Her heart-warming words neutralized my resentment of leaving the people with whom I was so closely knit and the environment that provided me with so much childhood pleasure and comfort.

"Do not stir, my child," Grandma Kamah told me, drawing me close to her. "May God go with you. May God guide and direct you. Trust in God." Then she added, "You will be educated. People of other races will come from faraway land and give you job." What that meant, I did not know. But as my life has unfolded, her prophetic words have remained with me.

When all the good-byes were said, Grandpa Dwah and I set out on our way. Because the road to Morblee, my father's birth town, was not accessible to cars in those days, we had to walk, a journey of about four hours. Grandpa wanted us to reach Morblee the same day, so he insisted that we walk fast. Also he would not let us stop to rest. I found it extremely difficult to keep up with Grandpa's grueling pace.

"John, *ah mu; ah nahn; bor ni ti ziahn!*" he repeatedly urged. "John, let's move on; let's walk; don't waste my time!"

Trying to keep up with his demands, I fell several times, cutting my knees and my toes. The more tired I got, the more frustrated and bitter I became. This was my first long-distance trip by foot. It was the first time I was regimented without regard for my feelings. I began to lag behind so I could make occasional stops without Grandpa's knowledge and get a little rest. When he did notice that I was trailing behind, he would shout, "John, *nyi ah ke mu!* John, come on, let's go."

"M-mni nyiehn," I would answer in an exhausted, shaky voice. "I -I'm coming."

As I struggled on, the contrast with the attitude of Grandpa Glor and Grandma Kamah became stronger. They had never scolded or spanked me, especially not for something beyond my ability. That didn't mean that they overlooked any negative behavior on my part. Whenever I misbehaved, they sat me down and advised me in a gentle manner. But they were persuasive, not regimental. They were tactful, not forceful—tenderhearted, not chiding.

Though I lacked their physical presence to encourage me, thinking of my grandparents helped me to forge on and not give in to self-pity. They had always wanted me to be successful and not allow myself to be defeated by harsh conditions.

The long, hectic trek finally came to an end when Grandpa Dwah and I arrived in Morblee at dusk. My father, Grandmother Chenda, and other relatives were on hand to welcome me. But no one showed any enthusiasm. There was none of the traditional welcome I was expecting. Grandmother Chenda didn't lift me onto her lap, chanting welcome slogans and songs of joy. My father didn't draw me close to him to ask me about my life in Whayongar Town.

I was now in a new environment, I reminded myself. It was different from Whayongar Town. It could be that Dad and Grandma Chenda were not the pampering type like Grandpa Glor and Grandma Kamah. So, trying to ignore the lack of traditional formalities, I gladly ate the delicious meal served me. After a warm bath, I went to bed and, overcome with fatigue, immediately fell asleep.

The next day, as expected, my father took me to Camphor Mission in Tubmanville Township, a Methodist institution about a twenty-five minutes' walk away, to begin my education. (Founded in 1947, the Mission was named for Bishop Alexander Camphor, a missionary from the United States.) For the first time I was setting foot on academic soil.

Now, I felt, I would be fulfilling the predictions of Grandma Kamah and the people of Whayongar Town who said that I would get a Western education. Even though I was too young to grasp exactly what a Western education was, those predictions were already becoming a driving force in my life.

Also for the first time, I met my younger brother, James. He was already a boarder at Camphor Mission, in the second grade. The fact that he, a younger brother, was ahead of me served as another propelling force, challenging me to follow his example.

My first impression of Camphor Mission was that it was basically a rural community, similar to Whayongar Town and Morblee. Like those towns, the campus was surrounded by high forest. It was not a very large campus, though. There were only three buildings—a church, a missionary residence, and a boys' dormitory, built close to each other on the small plot of ground that comprised the entire campus site. The church was roofed with corrugated iron sheets, while the other two buildings had thatch roofs. The clearing around the buildings was planted with a variety of crops, such as cassava, potatoes, and pineapples.

Camphor, as a Christian academic community, however, was different from other communities, as I soon learned. There was a serenity that greeted me on my arrival. The church was not only a place of worship; it was also used for the school. There were about eighty students, with girls in the minority. Most of the students were boarders, with the boys living in the dormitory and the girls sleeping in the home of the station superintendent. The off-campus students came from nearby towns and villages such as Gorgbahn, Baduahn, Joe Johnny Town, and Karngar Town. In addition to their academic work, the boys did the farm work. A portion of the crops produced was used to feed the students. The rest were sold in order to buy additional food.

When I arrived at Camphor, the Reverend Josiah F. Yancy and his wife, Hannah, were in charge of the Mission. They had come from Harper, the capital of Maryland County at the southeastern tip of Liberia. The Reverend Yancy was actually from Grand Bassa County, but his wife was a Marylander. They brought with them young James Dennis, now the Reverend James D. Karblee. The Reverend Yancy served in three capacities at that time. He was Superintendent of Group B District of the then Methodist Episcopal Church, he was the administrative head of Camphor School, and he was also the only teacher in the school, which ran from kindergarten to the eighth grade. His wife taught only when he was away on pastoral or related duties. Since one person could hardly be an effective teacher for so many students and so many grades, the senior students, who at that time were James Dennis, James Garjay, Samuel John, along with some others, helped teach the lower classes.

Before he returned to Morblee, Dad followed the advice of the Yancys by placing James and me in the care of a young fellow named Joe Garkpa. Joe was about fifteen years old and probably in the fourth grade. The Reverend and Mrs. Yancy gave Joe instructions on how to supervise our food and our laundry. Joe gladly accepted us, and from that moment on proved himself to be a sincere and reliable older "mission brother."

The staple foods at Camphor were cassava, breadfruit, and rice. Rice, though the national staple, was served just once a week, on Sunday. There was no central kitchen, so we had to cook our own meals. Not wanting us to eat plain boiled cassava or breadfruit, Joe would pound our slices into a nice dish of *dumboy*. (*Dumboy* is a dough made from boiled cassava, as well as other tubers and fruit such as eddoes, plantain, and breadfruits. The ingredients are pounded in a mortar, then molded by hand into rounded loaves and served with soup and sauce. *Dumboy* made from cassava is the principal dish of the Bahsors.) Joe always made sure that we did not go to bed hungry. He also took good care of our clothes. His dedicated love and care for us went beyond the bounds of being a mere "mission brother." James and I regarded him as a blood brother, because he actually substituted for one.

Pupils living on the Camphor campus were required to obey special rules that were considered necessary for their academic and social growth. One rule prohibited students from speaking the Bassa language on Sundays. The reason for this rule was that the national language of Liberia was officially English, and most of the teaching was done in English. But since Camphor Mission was in Grand Bassa County, a predominantly Bassa-speaking subpolitical region of Liberia, almost all the boarders spoke Bassa. This rule was established to help these students become used to speaking English. Violaters were punished by forced bed rest, or were made to haul water from the nearby creek.

This prohibition put me in quite a predicament. I had just come from Whayongar Town, where Bassa was the only language. What should I do? I could either try to speak English—which I didn't know—or remain mute on Sundays. I decided to remain silent. But when the other kids realized that I was silent because I didn't know English, they teased and made fun of me—without regard to the punishment I might undergo for disobeying the rule.

That first Sunday, Mettie, one of the Yancys' daughters, got me into trouble. Her constant teasing irritated me so much that I forgot my self-imposed sanction and called aloud, *"Ma, cheehn nouhn mar-yu nahn keh gbo-aye!"* "Ma, please advise these children!" What I really wanted to say was "Ma, please advise *this girl!*" Fortunately, Mrs. Yancy pitied my situation, and I wasn't punished.

The Yancys did their best to cater to the needs of the students, particularly those residing on campus. Mrs. Yancy was a gentle, caring, and loving person. She acted as a mother to all the students, not just her own children. I have kept in touch with her over the years, visiting her several times. She was alive and living with Mettie in Paynesville, near Monrovia, while this book was being written.

Chapter Three

From House Boy to Street Boy in Monrovia

My stay at Camphor Mission ended abruptly. After only a week and a half, my father came to take me away. He had arranged for me to live in Monrovia, Liberia's capital, and continue my schooling under the guardianship of a lady named Bonblayeh Jefferson, who had requested that I come live with her.

Again I was filled with resentment. I was just becoming acquainted with the other students. I had picked up a few English words and sentences, and soon, I knew, I would learn to speak English. I had a good brother in Joe Garkpa, who had been so nice to James and me. I wasn't sure that life in Monrovia would offer the same privileges.

But these thoughts were only the same futile struggle I had experienced less than two weeks earlier when I left Whayongar Town with Grandpa Dwah. Now the ultimate decision was Dad's—not mine—and it had already been made. So I had to give up my inner warfare and start on my second educational journey. After all, I reasoned, Dad was concerned about my education and he knew the right place for me to obtain it. Bonblayeh was a distant relative of Dad's. She had promised to help pay for my education while I lived with her.

For most of the journey to Monrovia, we had to walk. It took us two days to get to Firestone, where the highway from Monrovia ended. Firestone was a very large, multinational rubber plantation started in the early 1920s by Harvey S. Firestone, Jr., the American business tycoon. There we got a ride on a pickup truck bound for Monrovia.

Late on the third afternoon, we arrived at the Mechlin Street home of my guardian, opposite a large mosque (which is still intact). There I met Bonblayeh Jefferson and her four children, two girls and two boys: Mardeh, Mohndaymah, Tom, and Richard. Dad immediately turned me over to Bonblayeh, and she presented me to her daughter, Mardeh, with the words, "This is your son." When Mardeh later changed my name from John to Tommy, I was bewildered. But one thing was clear—I was her foster son from that moment on. I could not know that I wouldn't see or hear from my father for the next three years.

Mardeh enrolled me in the afternoon session of the Old Lady Crawford elementary school on Carey Street, just a few blocks away from my new home. I was told I was in the afternoon session because my guardian could not afford to register me in the school's morning classes. But later I wondered if the real reason was that she wanted me to work during the morning hours.

I didn't enjoy going to class in the afternoon. That is a general attitude in Liberia. Because most of the afternoon teachers also teach in the morning, it is assumed that they are not usually at their best after already having taught for five hours (8:00 A.M. to 1:00 P.M.). In addition, the students who attended morning schools made fun of those of us who went in the afternoon, so every student wanted to attend morning classes. For me, I soon discovered that my hectic life at Bonblayeh's, doing all the tasks assigned me, kept me so tired that it was almost impossible to pay attention in afternoon classes, especially since all classes were taught in English. With little encouragement and no easing up on the work at home, I soon quit attending school.

One of my main assignments was to care for Mardeh's newborn baby girl, Barbara. That included feeding and bathing Barbara, doing the laundry, as well as other childcare activities. Barbara's father, Kaiser Knowlden, was a well-to-do businessman who lived on Randall Street, not too far from our house. He and Mardeh were not legally married. They were simply "loving," as this type of relationship is termed in Liberia.

The tasks given me by Mardeh were strange and challenging. I was born and bred in a rural setting where childcare and laundry and other such tasks were never given to small boys to perform. They were reserved for women, particularly mothers. But since I wanted an education, I accepted the new challenges. I paid a high price, however. Every time I made a mistake, I was harshly punished, most often by severe beatings.

One such merciless flogging was at the hands of Kaiser Knowlden. Mardeh asked me to take Barbara to his house for a visit one day. While we were there, Barbara soiled her diaper and some of the stool fell on the living room carpet. Mr. Knowlden became infuriated. Seizing a coiled electric wire, he gave me a terrible beating, creating cuts and bruises all over my body. Then he made me clean up the feces with my shirt!

In addition to my assigned household chores, I also became a secondary breadwinner for the home. There were days when we had no food to eat, so I was sent out to the dump sites and other places to collect empty beer bottles. When I got them home, I washed them thoroughly, and then carried them on my head to sell at the breweries several miles away. On the way home, I'd use the money to buy food for the household. Sometimes I also bought dishes and cooking utensils.

This life went on for a long time—almost three years. Everyone else in the house seemed to enjoy the results of my work. But no one ever showed any real interest in the fact that I was not in school, since I refused to attend the afternoon session. Neither Bonblayeh nor Mardeh seemed prepared to address this crucial issue. They made no attempt to encourage me or to enroll me in the morning session in appreciation for all the work I did for them. My father never checked up on me, and I didn't know how to get in touch with him.

It was in my third year with Bonblayeh that I began to consider other alternatives. I did want an education, and I had had enough of enslaving tasks and inhumane punishments. My first thought was to run away. That would provide a quick and easy solution to my desire not to live with the Jeffersons anymore. But run away where? My home in Grand Bassa was over one hundred miles away, and I didn't know the way back. In Monrovia, I didn't know any relative or acquaintance to turn to. And it was equally risky to loiter aimlessly in a large city. Then I remembered—my mother had moved to Monrovia two years after I was born. I could go to her. But, would she accept me? Would she risk incurring my father's displeasure?

What should I do?

It was September 1959 when I made up my mind at last. I would run away, but I'd stay in Monrovia. I had by this time learned to speak English (the official language of Liberia) well enough to get along. First, I would go from house to house and beg any kindhearted person to take me on as a servant and send me to school. Second, I would use my running away to force my guardian, Bonblayeh, to send me back home.

I woke up early the next morning in high spirits, ready to put my plan to work. In the kitchen I began fumbling with the buckets, making it look as though I was already starting my chores. But as soon as the coast was clear, I escaped through the back of the house and went off into the streets. After wandering around a bit, I decided to visit the cemetery on Center Street to watch the boys play soccer. There, to my joy, I was asked to play on a team. One of the boys befriended me because I was a good goalkeeper. When the game ended late in the evening, he invited me to spend the night with him and his friends. Together we went down to Waterside, the economic center of Monrovia at that time.

In a large abandoned commercial building there, he introduced me to his buddies. "He's come to spend the night," he told them.

"He's not a part of us," an older boy objected, "he's a stranger." When my friend pleaded with him to reconsider, the fellow spoke with a note of authority. "I'm the boss here, and I say *no*."

The uncompromising gang leader had decided my fate. I had to leave and find lodging elsewhere. It was then about nine o'clock, and the idea of going home was ruled out. Eventually I sneaked into a newly constructed store in the city center and spent the night there.

In the morning, I rejoined my friends at the graveyard, where we played soccer until midday, then dispersed to find food. Play resumed in the afternoon, and in the evening we scattered to find places to sleep.

Gradually I became accustomed to my new life. I slept in odd places. I ate by working for different folks who paid me, sometimes with food, sometimes with money. Often I went without food. At times the group cooked a meal together. That was when I discovered one of my new friends could steal, and that the money he stole was sometimes used to buy our food. He was very good at what we called "table lifting," stealing money from the tables where women were displaying their wares. One day I watched him in action. While he asked a market woman about the prices of different commodities, pointing with one hand first in one direction then another, his other hand was skillfully maneuvering under the bag where the lady kept the money from her sales. He made away with four dollars.

After a couple of days the fellow took me to the market and told me, "Today it's your turn to take from under a table." Dumbfounded, I stood frozen with fear. "Get going," he insisted. "You must take your turn." With a throbbing heart and trembling hands I made an attempt, but came out with only eighty cents. "You're nothing but a stupid coward," he told me scornfully. "Now watch and see how it's done."

This time, however, he was caught in the act. "Rogue! Thief!" shouted the woman in the usual city theft-alert cry.

A mob quickly gathered around him and began to beat him rather brutally.

My fear redoubled. This supposedly expert con artist was now just a common criminal at the mercy of an angry mob. And I, too, had just been involved in a criminal act. Guilt and fear and the desire not to be nabbed as an accomplice made me take to my heels, and I got as far away from the market as I could. I would never have anything more to do with the thief, I decided, nor with any other member of the gang. I would go solo in my wayward life, I promised myself, in order to avoid the temptation of becoming a criminal. I would continue my usual house-to-house visits, offering service for food. And I would go on sleeping in abandoned buildings.

In the days that followed I was often hungry and had to beg for food. The runaway life was not without its danger. One night in central Monrovia a strange woman rushed toward me, cut my right arm with a sharp object, and kept on running without looking back. Blood ran down my arm into my hand for quite a while before I got the flow stopped. Fortunately the wound did not get infected. That experience made me even more careful and wary.

Early one morning I noticed my foster mother, Mardeh, coming in my direction. Not wanting her to see me, I ran to the back of a house where I hid until she was out of sight. If she had seen me, she would certainly have raised an alarm for me to be arrested by the police. I would have either been taken home and flogged or else placed in police custody.

Twice during my runaway time, I did try to take refuge with my mother, Conwree, who was living in Monrovia. But both times she brought me back to my guardians. Just as I had suspected, she was afraid of my father's wrath. So I continued to try to find someone not related to me to help me get an education.

One day I crossed the bridge over the Du (Mesurrado) River that links downtown Monrovia with the suburban district of Bushrod Island. In Vai Town, the first community on Bushrod after the bridge, I walked into the house of a man and begged his permission to live with him as a ward so that he could send me to school. At first the man seemed impressed by the bluntness of my appeal, yet he was hesitant. After a few minutes of consideration, he cautiously consented to my request, invited me in, and offered me some food.

Early the next morning he asked me to come with him to buy my school requirements. Happily, I agreed, only to find it a clever setup. Instead he took me to police headquarters (located on the site of the present Finance Ministry), and turned me over to the police on duty. "This boy came to me at my house last evening," he told them, "and begged me to let him stay with me so I could send him to school. I do sympathize with him and would love to help. But the problem is that I don't know his people or where he's from. I want you to locate his people, if that's possible." With these words he walked away, leaving me alone to face interrogation by the police.

Did I have relatives in Monrovia? the police asked. Yes, I told them. Where did my guardians live? They lived just a few blocks away from police headquarters, on the same street. Would I take them there? Yes, I said.

When we got to the house, Bonblayeh and Mardeh immediately began to express their disgust with me. I was ungrateful and disrespectful, they said, because I'd run away with no good reason. The police gave their account of how I got to police headquarters and left me with my guardians. Infuriated, Bonblayeh and Mardeh proceeded to give me a ferocious beating. Not satisfied with that, they threw me into the yard's pit toilet. Their inhumane treatment later reminded me of a proverb current at the time in Liberia: "The tender mercy of a heathen is cruelty!"

I'd been in the stinking pit for about forty-five minutes when I heard someone say with a note of pity, "That boy is somebody's child. Let's get him out of that nasty, foul-smelling latrine." Thinking back on it later, I wondered if one of Bonblayeh's other children had taken pity on me. As a rule Tom, Richard, and the youngest daughter, Mohndaymah, had been very nice to me because I had tried to serve them as well as their older sister.

But as soon as I was taken out of the latrine I was escorted back to police headquarters and put in a cell with several men and a boy about my age. I immediately made friends with the boy. Our friendship helped make the time in the crowded cell somewhat less unpleasant. I must say, in fairness to my guardians, that despite their latest treatment of me, they made sure to feed me in prison with food they prepared at home. That food helped cement the relationship between my prison friend and me because I always shared it with him. We also shared food with other prisoners.

I spent four days in police detention before my guardians agreed to have me released. Happy at being set free, I was even happier to learn that they had decided to send me back to my father! Finally I would be able to go to school!

Despite the Jeffersons' inability or unwillingness to enroll me in a desirable school, their subjecting me to hard and tedious tasks, and their occasional mistreatment of me, I must say that they did exhibit some humane qualities. They fed, clothed, and sheltered me, enabling me to stay with them for the best part of three years. I'm thankful, too, that while I was living with them, I learned to speak English.

But I really wanted an education.

Chapter Four

Back to Grand Bassa and Camphor

The time had come at last. I was going back to my father in Grand Bassa County. I was ready to leave right away, and was especially happy to learn that I wouldn't have to walk back to Morblee. My guardians had arranged with the captain of a sailboat, Captain Yahway, to take me to Bassa.

The idea of going on a boat caused me some uneasiness, however. It was scary to think of being on a small boat on the broad expanse of the Atlantic Ocean, particularly when I didn't know how to swim. But when I compared a boat trip to staying in Monrovia, my reluctance quickly melted away. Life here had become more fearsome than being in a tiny vessel on a vast body of water.

That same morning, Bonblayeh took me to Captain Yahway at the pier to begin my voyage back home. I bade the Jeffersons a pleasant good-bye and boarded the vessel with the other passengers. As we sailed out of the harbor, I sighed with relief and cast a good-riddance look at Monrovia, watching the buildings and landscape of the city fade away in the distance.

The bitter memories, however, were not so easy to get rid of. I began to go back over the ordeal I had passed through: the laborious household chores; the beatings, particularly the sheer brutality of Kaiser Knowlden; the risky and dehumanizing life of being a runaway; the jailing. Most of all I regretted the precious time wasted without going to school.

Though I tried to blame most of my ordeal on fate, I knew that I could never compromise my need for education. That would be a betrayal of the high expectations of Grandma

Kamah, Grandpa Glor, and the folk of Whayongar Town—as well as the expressed will of my father. Now that I was returning to Dad I was still confident that he would send me to school.

Captain Yahway and the crew were kindly seafarers. They offered me food and made sure I was comfortable. Their concern helped to further revive my spirit. After a few days of sailing, we docked in Buchanan City. There Captain Yahway took me to his house and introduced me to his family. They gladly welcomed me and lovingly cared for me during my two weeks with them. Their kindness motivated me to try to help with the daily activities of the home. I also regularly went to the beach to help the Ghanaian fishermen haul in their nets and their fish, and pull their canoes on shore. When we'd finished, they would pay me with fish, which I brought home to the Yahways for food.

After two weeks, Captain Yahway asked his mother-in-law, Mehnsleh, who lived in a rural area in the direction of Morblee, to take me to my father. Mehnsleh was in her fifties or sixties and was related in some way to Dad. I was glad to accompany her, figuring it was better to be in school in a rural setting than to waste my time in the city. I would rather become an educated person from the country than to remain an idiot from the city.

But Mehnsleh did not take me straight to my father. Instead, she took me to her home in Darwein. From there she sent a message to him in Morblee asking him to come and get me. He did not come immediately, and later I was told that he was away attending a church meeting. While I waited, I became quite friendly with a boy named Solomon and even helped him clear a parcel of land so he could plant cassava. Mother Mehnsleh was a kind person and provided me with food for the time I was in her home.

After a few days, my father returned to Morblee from his trip and sent two of my aunts, Titi and Kpayehwheh, to Darwein to get me. In Morblee I happily greeted my father, but instead of a welcome, I got an angry response. "You!

You wasted your time in Monrovia! You didn't go to school. You will never be educated. You'll always be a vagabond and a burden to your younger brother, James." James was now in the fourth grade.

Even though I kept trying to tell him that my guardians did not take a serious interest in my schooling, Dad didn't believe me. He assumed that I had been attending school and decided to test me by asking me to recite the alphabet. When I failed the test, he became so enraged that he flogged me hard and demanded that I learn the alphabet that night. It soon became apparent that I wasn't going to make it, and he beat me for the second time. The beating became so severe and unbearable that I ran from the room.

My brother, James, who had been watching all this time, began to cry. With tears in his eyes, he walked up to me. "John," he said in a compassionate voice, "I will help you." The next day we found a quiet, shady spot at the edge of town to use as a classroom. Miraculously, it seemed, with James's help, I learned not only to recite the alphabet but also to read the entire *Royal Primer,* Book I, in just two days! And, at the same time, I learned the multiplication tables, the Roman numerals, and some other pregrade requirements. Over the next weeks, James continued to help me master the pregrade work. I owe James a deep debt of gratitude for his help. Not only did he save me from Dad's wrath, but he also gave me a foretaste of the one thing I was yearning for—an education.

All this happened in December 1959. The school year had just ended and it was now vacation time. December, January, and February are summer months in Liberia.

In March 1960, my father registered me again at Camphor Mission. I would be in the first grade and I was eleven years old. Now at last I was actually beginning the academic journey I had long dreamed of. This time James and I didn't live on campus, but in Morblee, and we walked to school along with several other boys from the village. These included my uncle Alfred Dwah, and my cousins

John Zeehwon, John Mason Kayfoain, James Mason Kayfoain, Joshua David, and Daniel Glay. My aunts Titi, Kpayehwheh, and Yonnonkplen were not permitted to attend school, nor was my girl cousin Gbehzohnmah. The Bassa people believed that Western education was not meant for girls.

In the three years I had been in Monrovia, the leadership at Camphor had changed. The Reverend Yancy had died, and his wife and children had moved to Monrovia. The Earlys were now in charge. Mrs. Annie Early was the school's principal. Her husband, the Reverend J. Cephas Early, Sr., was district superintendent and station manager. The Earlys were to play a very meaningful role in my life. Almost immediately they began to motivate and inspire me to press forward with my education. At times they also helped pay my school fees.

The church building at Camphor was still being used for classes. The atmosphere on the campus was conducive for learning and I was able to adapt easily. I also made many new friends, some of whom—like Solomon Glay, Josiah Zeehwon, Joshua Glay, and Isaac Glay—became very special to me. Unlike my wayward buddies in Monrovia, we all shared a common interest, getting an education, and our conversations focused on our school activities and classes. None of us ever dared to violate the rules governing the conduct of students during and after school hours.

The encouraging environment at Camphor helped me excel in my lessons. But almost immediately I was confronted with a challenge. There was a textbook required for first-grade reading, *On Four Feet,* and each student had to have his own copy. But the price was U.S. $1.50—an amount difficult for every student, including myself, to come up with. Suddenly I had a bright idea. I would take a Friday off to cut palm and would sell the nuts for cash.

That Friday morning, I got a machete and went into the bush to look for ripe palm nuts. But halfway up the first tree, my bamboo ladder broke and I fell with a bang, landing on my back on the hard ground, with my left hip almost out of joint. The pain was terrible; all I could do was lie there for quite a long time. Eventually the pain subsided and I was able to get up. With massage and exercise I managed to get my hip back in position. But I wasn't going to give up. I was still determined to cut the palm, so I got another ladder, climbed rather clumsily up the tree, and cut the two bunches of nuts that were ripe.

The following day, with the palmnuts on my head, I walked to Buchanan City, sold the nuts, and bought a copy of *On Four Feet*. The book became one of my early school treasures—a treasure I shared with the other students, who weren't able to get their own copies. We were all able to make good use of it because the school administration relaxed its previous rule that every student had to have his own copy.

At Camphor I was blessed with teachers who built a strong academic and spiritual foundation for me from the first through the sixth grades. These included the Earlys, Joseph Shelton, John Smith, James Spiller, James G. Yarr, and the Reverend William K. Bobbroh. While he was at Camphor, the Reverend Bobbroh was married to Martha Page, the daughter of the Reverend Alfred Page, pastor of the Camphor church at the time.

The teachers also helped mold my character and give me a sense of direction. The commitment of the Reverend Bobbroh was particularly outstanding. By the time I got to the sixth grade, I was the only student, and the Reverend Bobbroh devoted much of his time to preparing me to pass the national exam, which was a prerequisite for promotion to junior high school. He encouraged me to persevere and press forward in my educational pursuit. The future was bright, he kept telling me, for those who were prepared for it.

I will always remember these teachers with gratitude for their part in my education. Without them, whatever accomplishments I have achieved might not have been possible.

They are all dead now, but the knowledge they passed on to me and the patient love they showed me have helped carry me through the years.

While I was a student at Camphor, I became an active member of the Camphor Memorial Methodist Church (now the Garfield UMC). Over the years, the ministers taught us God's moral guidelines and showed us God's plan of salvation, providing spiritual awareness to students who had little or no knowledge of the gospel. These dedicated men of the Camphor Church urged us to study and live by the Word of God. This, they reminded us, was the basic reason why the school was established. One of the church leaders during my years at Camphor was the Reverend George Goodside Dean, regarded as the father of Methodism among the Bassa ethnic group of Liberia. Other leaders were the Reverend Alfred W. Page, the Reverend David J. Glay, and the Reverend David Mason. The Reverend Mason was my father's cousin. His mother, Yoh, was Grandpa Dwah's sister, and he lived in Morblee when he pastored the church at Camphor.

After four years of study and hard work it was time to celebrate. My graduation from the sixth grade came in December 1964, after I had successfully passed the national exam. In those four years, I had received two double promotions. The graduation ceremonies were a time of joy and celebration, not only for students, but also for parents, guardians, relatives, teachers, and friends. I was especially grateful to the Reverend and Mrs. Early. The joy and pride they showed in my accomplishments gave me the feeling that I was their own son.

My brother James, who had left Camphor two years before, came back to campus, not wanting to miss the ceremonies. When I saw him, I embraced him heartily and thanked him for spending time to give me such a good foundation for my education. He expressed his pride in me for the strides I had made in these four years. In fact, I was now just one grade behind him, rather than two, because of my promotions.

Many of my relatives came to the graduation ceremonies. My cousin James Yarr had been one of my teachers at Camphor, encouraging me to take my learning seriously. My uncles Levi Russell, Big Borbor, and Small Borbor, as well as Mother's uncle Gbor Clinton had not only provided me with moral guidance, but also with financial assistance. I was very sad, though, that neither my mother nor my maternal grandmother, Kamah, came to the ceremonies. They had not been told of the event. Equally sad was the absence of Grandpa Glor. He would have greeted my graduation with joy. Unfortunately, he had died two years earlier.

My father also did not come for the occasion. He was away on business for the church. When he did return, however, he expressed his delight and commended me for my achievement. Then he asked, "Do you now realize my reason for scolding you and beating you? It was because I wanted you to be educated."

For the first time it dawned on me that my father had not meant to harm me with his beatings. He had a burning desire for me to be educated, otherwise he would not have registered me at Camphor. And he had not objected when James volunteered to teach me on that painful day of my arrival in Morblee. Now, the harsh methods he had used had finally paid off. Here I was, a cheerful graduate, and my Dad was a proud father. The scoldings, the beatings, the bruises, the pains, the times of disillusionment had turned into moments of pride, joy, and celebration. Even before I talked to my father, I had selected the theme "Perseverance" for my graduation speech.

It wasn't until a few years later that I came to understand the background for the methods Dad employed to induce me to learn. As I mentioned earlier, my father was a product of the Ward System, in which indigenous tribal boys were sent to live with Americo-Liberian or Congo settler families in order to be educated in a Western, "Christian" manner. Unfortunately, the system had serious drawbacks. Corporal and negative punishments were the normal means of trying to force tribal Liberians to become assimilated into the more Western culture of the coastal cities. So scolding, bullying, and beating were basic methods used in the educational process, with the intention of inducing learning.

From my later study of psychology, I have learned that environmental factors, particularly such negative ones as corporal punishment and scolding, can have a lasting detrimental impact on people. I believe that this was my father's predicament. I, too, fell victim to the same scenario when I returned to teach at Camphor after completing high school. I also used the same methods in bringing up my older children. It wasn't until my eyes were opened in my studies at Teacher's College that I changed my ways.

Sadly, the practice still exists in Liberia, in schools, homes, the government, the church, and in almost every stratum of our national life. I don't believe that statement is an exaggeration. True, nobody beats or flogs anybody else in the government or the church. On the other hand, any statement or action, whether by ordinary people or by leaders in or out of the government and the church, that has the potential of hurting or abusing others socially, economically, politically, morally, or spiritually, is tantamount to beating them. The beatings may be symbolic. The resulting painful feelings, though not physical, are real.

I am happy to say that I never experienced harsh treatment at Camphor. But the negative methods of imparting knowledge that I did encounter would take a long time to correct, and for the time being, they became a part of my seeking a better life through education. Most of all, however, I believed that my success in graduating from elementary school was a manifestation of God's goodness—God's continued love, care, and guidance through the people who made my stay at Camphor rewarding.

Chapter Five

High School in Buchanan City

Graduation at Camphor was over. The excitement was past. But two things remained from my four years there. One was the positive feeling of self-worth resulting from my academic achievement. The other was a fiery urge to continue my education.

Dad and I agreed that I should move to Lower Buchanan to attend high school. Now called Buchanan City, this seaport city is the capital of Grand Bassa County. In the two summer months (January and February) after graduation, I made several trips to the capital to settle on a place to live. My brother James was already going to school there, living in the home of the Reverend George Mingle, the pastor of Whitfield Memorial MC. When I told James that I wanted us to live together, we decided to talk to three of Dad's female cousins to see if they'd be willing to help us. Wheaygba Sherman, Gbonzu Montgomery, who was Wheaygba's daughter, and Popo Sherman gladly accepted our appeal, and provided a room for us in one of Cousin Popo's houses. Cousin Popo, whom we called Aunt Popo, owned two houses on either side of a house owned by Gbonzu. Although Cousin Wheaygba had her own house a few blocks away, she was living with her daughter.

So in February 1965, I moved to Buchanan City and enrolled in seventh grade at Bassa High School. James left the Mingles' house and joined me at Aunt Popo's. He had already had a year in high school after graduating from the sixth grade at the Bassa Elementary Demonstration School. We had an easier time getting to school than we had had in

Morblee. There it had taken us almost an hour to walk from Morblee to Camphor Mission. But Bassa High School was less than five minutes from our new home. So we wouldn't have to expend a lot of energy to be on time, and the rainy season (mid-April to mid-October) wouldn't pose any threat on our way to and from school.

James had a number of friends and classmates who also became my friends, among them Charles Walker Brumskine, and Bobby and Gentry Perry. Some time later, Roland Giahyu, another cousin of ours, joined us in boarding at Cousin Popo's. James and I also made friends with our neighbors, especially the boys our age who lived in the home of Father Daniel G. Harris. Father Harris was the priest of St. Mary's Episcopal Church in Buchanan City. Three of the boys with whom we became quite intimate were Benjamin Harris (now Zehyu Wuduorgar),[1] James Travers, and Joseph Tarr. Ben and James were students at the Seventh Day Adventist School. After he finished the eighth grade, Ben joined us at Bassa High, where I was now a sophomore and James a junior. James Travers started Bassa High a year after I graduated. Since we were all around the same age, we supported and encouraged each other in our studies, and for the most part we got on very well together.

The older boys in Father Harris's house became like big brothers to us and helped to motivate us. James Harris and John Tarr were eleventh and tenth graders at Bassa High. Joe Harris and David Teague worked with LAMCO, an iron ore mining company that was a joint venture involving the Liberian government together with American and Swedish investors. Its several thousand employees included Liberians and non-Liberians. I was a student worker there myself during two summer vacations, earning money for school. One summer I worked in the refrigerator and air-conditioner repair department. Another summer I worked with the heavy-duty department.

Joe and David were generous to us high school students. They would quite often give us money when they received their salaries, helping us to meet some of our needs. Two other employees of LAMCO lived in Aunt Popo's house and were also good to us. Togba Davis and Julius Aryee, for whom I did laundry on weekends, never forgot to pay me.

Bassa High had a committed and competent group of administrators and teachers concerned with turning us into good and honorable citizens. Most of them had bachelors degrees while few had masters degrees and diplomas. The principal, Philemon E. Harris, was a strong disciplinarian, generally uncompromising on matters of principle. The leadership of "Joe Prince," as he was affectionately called, made Bassa High one of the most outstanding and respected institutions in the county and in the country, a true *Turis Lucis*, "Tower of Light"—the school motto. Philip V. Saywrayne as vice principal, Edward J. Harris, registrar and dean of admissions, and Bertha Delmeda, academic dean, also served as faculty members. (In appendix 2 I have listed the rest of the faculty members with gratitude.)

In addition to our regular classes, Bassa High offered a number of extracurricular activities. As a member of the drama club, which was noted for staging Christian-oriented plays, I was often selected to play the part of a pastor, a fact that earned me the nickname "Rev Innis." I enjoyed playing soccer, and in our annual interclass soccer tournament when I was in tenth grade, I played the number eleven position for my class. Besides taking part in the ROTC program on campus, I was also a member of the school's team for the "Meet the Challenge" annual academic competition. This was a nationwide event carried live over both national radio and television. In my senior year, I became president of the student government. Our class presented a sofa set to the school's administration and faculty in gratitude for their part in our education. (In appendix 2 I list some of my classmates from my six years at Bassa High.) Our class sponsor was Mrs. Helen Summerville.

All through high school, I was also actively involved in Christian activities. I joined Whitfield Memorial UMC where I served as recording secretary, sang in the choir, and was an active leader of the youth fellowship (UMYF), eventually serving as president. As members of the UMYF we conducted Bible studies, participated in worship services, visited the sick, and carried out a major cleanup campaign at the church. We also raised money for needy students at Camphor Mission.

Many of our high school and church young people also became active in the Buchanan branch of Youth for Christ (YFC). Youth for Christ in Liberia was started in Monrovia by missionaries serving with the Christian radio station ELWA (Eternal Love Winning Africa). YFC's main thrust was evangelism among and by young people. One activity it sponsored was a yearly Bible contest, "Teen Time Quiz," in which junior and senior high students from Monrovia and elsewhere demonstrated their knowledge of the Bible. YFC was started in Buchanan City by the Reverend Abba G. Karnga, a former staff member of ELWA, when he came to be principal of the government elementary demonstration school. We held our own Teen Time Quiz in Buchanan City, for which I was Quizmaster. Some of our top quizzers are named in appendix 2.

The Reverend Karnga was and is a visionary leader. His commitment to the spiritual, moral, and educational development of young people led to the formation of the Christian Education Foundation of Liberia (CEF). The foundation's goal is to foster unity among the churches in Grand Bassa, and to promote education. In 1969 this dream led to the establishment of the Christian High School—which became the second high school in Grand Bassa County at the time.

Even though I worked in the summer to earn money, I would not have been able to finish high school without the help of many people. My father was a public school teacher. To supply me with the finances I needed, he established a legal power of attorney arrangement (usually referred to by its initials, LPA), with Mohammed Ali, a Lebanese merchant in Buchanan City, so I could obtain cash and other essential items. LPAs were popular business arrangements at the time, more or less filling the role of banks. Low-income government employees would mortgage their salary checks to Lebanese businesses or other businesses for goods or cash in advance. The 10 percent charged by the merchants was exploitative, but the system did help folk take care of financial needs as well as cope with unexpected emergencies.

My mother also sent food, as well as a meager allowance whenever she could afford it. *Gari* was one dish she often sent, which is made from the tubers of the cassava tree. The cousins with whom we lived prepared meals for us on a daily basis. James's mother, Nida, also helped us out at times, as did my uncles Borbor and Levi, and my cousin James Yarr.

We became good friends with Nathan, John, Joe, James, and Reuben Mingle, the sons of the Reverend George Mingle with whom my brother James used to live. Nathan was James's and my best friend, and he taught me to ride a motorcycle. When he worked for Liberia Agriculture Company in Grand Bassa County, Nathan helped both James and me financially. Later, Nathan became a UMC minister and district superintendent. I was his best man when he married Rosetta Johnson. Sadly, he died while I was working in the United States. I was unable to return to Liberia for his funeral, but my son Youjay was there to represent us. His death touched us very deeply and we still miss him.

The St. John River District of the UMC also gave both James and me financial help at times for which we were very grateful.

Another friend whose kindness I will always remember is Anita Doegbee. Anita was in the class ahead of me, and after she graduated she gave me her set of twelfth grade textbooks free of charge—a real gift both financially and educationally.

For six years I worked hard. Finally it was graduation time. But my joy evaporated when I realized I was going to have to miss the ceremonies. I didn't have the money to buy the clothes I needed. It would take U.S. $100 to buy two suits, a blue and a gray, as well as shirts and neckties to match the suits, and shoes, for the baccalaureate and commencement exercises. In addition, I had to rent a gown. I was already feeling very depressed when James Howard, one of my classmates, came to the house so we could start on our prearranged trip to Monrovia to buy our clothes. Too ashamed to admit to James that I didn't have the money, I merely said, "Go ahead, James. I'll follow later."

James had no sooner left than I burst into tears. Aunt Popo and Cousin Wheaygba heard me sobbing and came into my room to ask me what was wrong. "Calm down," they told me after I had explained the situation. "You've been so helpful, John, particularly since your brother graduated and moved away. You haven't been proud. You've worked for us with no frown on your face. And you've regarded us as your own parents. So we have to show our appreciation for the way you have loved and respected us. We want you to have thirty-five dollars to help you buy your clothes."

Their generosity and kind words touched me deeply. They not only helped cheer me up, but they also moved me to action. I went round to other relatives and acquaintances, and with their generous help I got enough money so that I was able to go to Monrovia to buy what I needed. My mother gave me the money for one shirt by getting the money on credit from a kind lady. Cousin James Yarr got me the other shirt on Sunday morning, the day of commencement, from John Azzam, a Lebanese merchant with whom he had an LPA.

So it was with great joy and thankfulness that I was able to take part in the graduation ceremonies with my four classmates: James Howard, Betty Mason, Isabella Brown, and Christiana Duncan. It was quite different from my graduation from sixth grade at Camphor, where I was the only one in my class. Being able to share this happy time after years of working together made the occasion even more meaningful. Another joy was that my mother, Conwree, was able to attend the ceremonies, along with my brother, James. Cousins Popo, Wheaygba, Gbonzu, and James Yarr were there as well.

I had graduated, not only through my own hard work, but also through the love and care that family members, relatives, and many others had shown me.

Note

1. Boys who were sent to live with settler families often took the surname of that family, as did my father. Many of them, after they were adults, resumed their original indigenous names: for example, James Dennis became James D. Karblee.

Chapter Six

Sharing Knowledge and Earning Money for College

I still had a burning desire to continue my education. That meant enrolling at the University of Liberia where my brother James was now a sophomore in the College of Agriculture and Forestry. But I had no money and the possibility of funds or sponsorship was remote. Both James and I had been recommended for scholarships from the Liberia Annual Conference of the UMC, thanks to the Reverend J. Cephas Early, Sr. But the process was too slow. James's scholarship, based primarily on his active involvement with the Conference's youth programs, didn't come through until his second year, and he had to raise his own funds for his freshman year.

My second option was to teach at the Camphor Mission School. Since it seemed unlikely that any funds for a university education would be immediately available, I settled for my second choice. Yet, the decision to teach at Camphor was not made wholly on financial grounds. If I'd wanted to make good money, I would have applied to LAMCO, the giant iron ore company that was at the peak of its operations in Buchanan City. This would have not only have given me better pay but also provided more material benefits than teaching at Camphor. One reason I decided to return to Camphor was to show my appreciation for the founding fathers and mothers, for their vision, sacrifice, and dedication that brought the Mission into being. Camphor had started me on my educational and spiritual journeys and I wanted to help keep the vision alive for others.

My second reason for deciding to go back to Camphor was to share the knowledge I had acquired at high school. As an alumnus of the school, I felt it incumbent on me to help the young people from rural Bassaland and other areas of the nation. My application to the Division of General Education of the UMC in Monrovia was accepted, and in March 1971, I officially joined the faculty of Camphor Mission. I was given living space on the campus and brought with me my brother, Nathaniel Innis, my mother's son, to get him further along on his educational journey. Nathaniel was in the second grade.[1]

When I returned to Camphor I found that Mrs. Annie Early was no longer principal of the school but had become headmistress of the Mission. Her primary area of responsibility was the welfare and discipline of the boarding students. The new principal and chief administrative head of the Mission was Alvin Thomas. As the one responsible for maintaining a positive learning environment, his job was to work together with the teachers and other administrative staff, as well as to take charge in emergency situations. Because Mr. Thomas did not live at the Mission, but in Buchanan City, about fifteen miles from Camphor, it sometimes fell to the rest of us teachers to work with the students to solve their problems.

My responsibilities as the homeroom teacher for the fourth, fifth, and sixth grades kept me exceedingly busy. I not only had to teach these three classes all the required subjects, but I also had to help the sixth graders prepare for the National Exams. Grades 3 and 4 met together in one room. Grades 5 and 6 met together in another. To keep the students occupied simultaneously on a daily basis, I had to plan not only the lessons but also the strategies for presentation, to keep everyone interested.

A number of my students were committed to the learning process. Josiah Zeehwon, who later was ordained as the Reverend Alexander Boe[2] was one of those. So was my brother, Nathaniel. Others were Adolphus Junius, Joseph

Thomas, and Joseph Gaye. Joseph Gaye was my special student. Though he was not a fast learner like the others, he had a strong desire to learn and was determined and eager to achieve his goal. In some ways he reminded me of myself when I was at Camphor. What impressed me more about him, though, was his positive character. He helped to pay for his room and board by working for Nathaniel and me. He cooked for us—there was still no general kitchen or dining room for the school and each person was responsible for cooking his or her own food—and doing laundry and other jobs, always with a respectful and caring attitude. He also kept track of all my money, and proved very trustworthy.

In addition to the regular academic responsibilities, I involved myself with the students in both sporting and religious activities. I wanted to be in the position of "big brother" to them, to create a bond of belonging and also to cultivate positive values. Soccer and kickball were our two leading sports. Our group engaged in evangelism among the young people in the surrounding areas. We visited and prayed with the elderly, and we provided village-to-village community services.

During my two years of teaching at Camphor, I kept in touch with my own village of Whayongar Town and my people there, and also was able to make periodic visits to my father and relatives at Morblee. I was also very active with the Camphor Memorial UMC, and became the church's youth leader. I did not let this position interfere with my main job as a teacher, because I continued to feel my obligation to share the knowledge I had acquired with my rural brothers and sisters.

Notes

1. It is part of Bassa tradition that older family members and relatives become responsible for the younger members, caring for them and, where it is desired, helping them with their education. I talk more about this in chapter 17.
2. See note 1 in chapter 5.

Chapter Seven

Studying and Working at the University of Liberia

Beware of how you conduct yourself in society; because when society is about to decide your fate, you might not be present to defend or commend yourself.

—Philip V. Saywrene

Philip Saywrene, one of my instructors at Bassa High School, was very fond of giving this piece of advice to his students. It's a secular version of the biblical text, "Be not deceived; God is not mocked: for whatsoever a man soweth, that shall he also reap" (Galatians 6:7 KJV).

Both the quotation and the text can be interpreted either negatively or positively, and both are relevant to this chapter, because they relate to the circumstances that enabled me to enter the University of Liberia.

It did not occur to me during the two years that I was teaching and also serving as youth leader for the Camphor Church, from 1971–1973, that my activities were being closely monitored by leaders in the Liberia Annual Conference (LAC). One of those leaders was Dale Epple, a United Methodist missionary and the Conference Youth Director. (He is now a minister in the West Ohio Conference.) As he evaluated my work with the young people at Camphor and in the church, he was convinced that I needed to continue my education. As a result he recommended to the scholarship committee of the LAC that I be awarded a scholarship to attend the University of Liberia. When the scholarship was approved, I promised the committee that after graduation I would return to Camphor to teach.

In order to be accepted at the university, I had to take the university placement exam covering English and mathematics. I passed the English part of the exam and was able to enroll in the William V. S. Tubman Teachers College,[1] but only as a remedial student, because I had not passed the math section. I soon cleared the deficiency in math, however, and was then eligible to take the full credit hours required by the college.

I started university in 1973 at the age of twenty-four. My brother James had also received a scholarship for 1972, his sophomore year in the Agriculture College. Though Dale Epple was the primary force behind our getting scholarships, I am sure that the Reverend J. Cephas Early's previous recommendations helped the committee's decisions. The Reverend Early told me that our getting the scholarships was a dream-come-true for him.

My scholarship was for U.S. $500 per year. That only took care of tuition and boarding. There were no provisions for books or for a stipend. Still, I was very grateful to the church for helping me obtain a college degree that would qualify me for improved service to society as well as to the church. I would have to improvise ways of meeting the rest of my needs. As a substitute for purchasing textbooks, I decided, I would rely on note taking and the library.

But my real problem was that in addition to needing money for personal items, such as toiletries and laundry soap, I was caring for my brother Nathaniel, and my sister Felicia had now joined us.[2] The more I thought about how much money I needed, the more depressed I got. I even contemplated quitting the university to find a job. When I told my friend Isabella Brown, with whom I had graduated from high school, about my decision to quit, she advised me strongly not to. Isabella had gone directly to University from Bassa High, so was now a junior. She shared with me her past struggles and the inner satisfaction she was experiencing as the result of her determination to face all odds.

So I did not quit. Instead, I hunted for a part-time job. Fortunately I was able to find one in the Youth Department of the UMC, as secretary to the Reverend Daniel G. Gueh, who was the director of the department. My monthly salary was U.S. $15. Two months later I applied to the church's Department of Education, headed by Methodist missionary Elwyn C. Hulett, and I was hired as an office attendant on the same part-time basis. My total salary was thus U.S. $30. This meager amount I used to pay for my school requirements and immediate personal needs.

I don't think I would have been able to manage financially—certainly I'd have been more stressed than I was—if the Reverend and Mrs. J. Cephas Early hadn't regularly augmented the small amount I was able to earn. I am forever grateful to them and to other friends and family members who helped meet my needs. I can't forget their generosity that made it possible for me to continue my studies at the university. (I name them in appendix 3.)

While I was working at the Department of Education, I met my dear friend Joseph C. S. Sagbe. He, too, had taught before he came to the university, at the Ganta United Methodist Mission in northern Liberia. He, too, was a recipient of a UMC scholarship. He and I participated in the preparation of a spelling book series produced for grades 1 to 6 in UMC schools. The editors were Elwyn Hulett, his wife Cynthia Hulett, and Margie Clay, a Peace Corps Volunteer assigned to the UMC Department of Education by the Ministry of Education of the Republic of Liberia. Sagbe and I remained in the department until the Reverend James Karmbor, a Liberian, replaced Elwyn as director.

Sagbe and I became very close. Because we roomed together in Simon Greenleaf Hall, the men's dorm on the campus, we nicknamed ourselves "roommates," and the name has remained with us. As office attendants, we would go to the Department of Education every day after school to correct the spelling series, scrub the office floors, and do whatever other jobs needed doing. We encouraged each other to do our jobs well and to attach equal importance to our studies. I acted as supervisor for our office work, making sure that we worked diligently and with humility, never leaving anything undone. And twice I was the spokesman when we appealed to the department head for an increase in our stipends—from thirty to fifty dollars per month.

Some of my studies I found tedious. I had a difficult time with two of the prerequisite courses, mathematics and physical geography. Math was never my strong suit, and I didn't have a good background in physical geography. To make matters worse, the geography instructor was German, and not fluent in English, so that I found it very difficult to understand him. By dint of hard work, though, I managed to pass both classes.

Classes in the areas of social science were much more congenial to me, and I got along well in them: history, political science, public administration, and psychology. I also enjoyed courses in the education department: the history of education, methodology, and practice teaching. I didn't score all A's in these subjects, but I did manage to get on the Honor Roll once with an average of 3.98.

I did not spend all my time in classes, studying, and working. I was very much involved with campus activities. One of them was the Bassa University Student Association, which I joined in 1974. Two years later I was elected association secretary, working with David Jallah who was president. In my senior year, I was elected association president, and one of my former classmates at Bassa High, Emmanuel Reeves, was vice president. Emmanuel and I respected each other and worked well together. The association worked to promote unity among the Bassa students at the university. We always reminded our members never to forget Grand Bassa County, our place of origin.

One of the ways we kept in touch with Grand Bassa County was by establishing a good working relationship with the county's leaders, including the Honorable Joseph M. N. Gbadyu, county superintendent, and with the legislative caucus.

I was not involved very much in campus politics, though nearly the whole student body participated in campus political activities. There were two leading student parties, the All Students Alliance Party (ASAP) and the Student Unification Party (SUP), and they were divided on almost every social, ethnic, economic, and political issue. I was not, however, a member of either party. Not that I was insensitive to the plight of students at the university or to the general state of affairs in Liberia. But I was more concerned with the reasons for which I was at the university—to study hard, graduate, and fulfill my goal to return to rural Camphor Mission as a professional teacher. And I was more interested in finding concrete ways in which students could improve their academic lives and also become involved in volunteer services. For instance, there was a very real need for tutorial classes in many subjects, for literacy training, as well as various work projects both in Monrovia and elsewhere in the country. These activities should have been high on the platforms of the campus political parties. Instead, they focused on the policies and performance of the Liberian Government. My only involvement with them was to become friendly with the leaders of both parties.

Another part of my busy and crowded life involved my commitment to the church. In Monrovia I became an affiliate member of the J. J. Powell UMC. When I first joined that church, the Reverend David Tweh Toe was the pastor. The Reverend James D. Karblee succeeded him. I also remained involved with my home churches. During vacations, I always went home to have fellowship with my brothers and sisters either at Whitfield Memorial UMC in Buchanan City or at Camphor Memorial UMC.

Four busy and laborious years passed. I finished my practice teaching at B. W. Harris Episcopal High School, and was eligible for graduation. The news filled me with joy and pride. I had followed my friend Isabella's advice, I had stuck with it, and I had made it.

It seemed very special to me that our commencement speaker was the Reverend Dr. Bennie D. Warner, bishop of the UMC. He was also vice president of the Republic of Liberia under President William Tolbert. Just as special was the attendance of many of my family members, relatives, supporters, and friends, who were on hand to extend their appreciation and congratulations. But again, as on my graduation from high school, my father was absent. As secretary for the St. John River District of the UMC, he was responsible for preparations for the Annual Conference, which is usually held the second week in December, and so would take place almost immediately after the graduation ceremonies.

With my diploma in hand, I returned to Bassa from the graduation ceremonies to attend the District Conference. There my graduation was celebrated by the conference members with joy, and with a special ceremony. The Reverend and Mrs. Early were among those who helped to organize the program, which my father also attended.

"John," my father said to me, "I didn't mean any harm when I flogged and scolded you about your education. I wanted for you to become someone useful. I am sorry that I beat you rather than being calmer and persuasive. But my dream for you has become a reality. Today I'm proud to have a determined son like you." Embracing me, he told me with tears, "John, you've made it!"

Unable to hold back my emotions, I too burst into tears. I understood again that, indeed, my father had not meant any harm. Only because I had borne the lashes and the scoldings had I been able to reach this far. Now I had something of value to offer my brothers and sisters, my parents, my relatives, my church, and Liberian society. But none of that would have been possible if I had disrespected my father by running away the day he flogged me, vowing never to go to school.

I thanked the members of the District Conference for their spiritual, moral, and financial support. "Without your prayers and total help," I told them, "I could not have made it thus far." As the conference offered a prayer of thanksgiving for my achievement, I felt spiritually refreshed. Their expressions of Christian love and joy for my achievement had deeply touched me.

Notes

1. Named in honor of William V. S. Tubman, president of Liberia from 1944 until his death in 1971.
2. Felicia is my mother's daughter.

Chapter Eight

Expanding Horizons at Camphor Mission

The day before I graduated from college, David Jallah, a broadcaster at the station, interviewed me on ELBC, the radio station of the Liberian Broadcasting Corporation. Dave was a former president of the Grand Bassa University Student Association and had graduated a year or two before me. "John," Dave asked me, "now that you are about to graduate from the University of Liberia, what are your plans?"

My answer was clear and unequivocal. "I'm going back home to work with the rural masses in Grand Bassa County," I told him, "especially those at Camphor United Methodist Mission. I am committed to share my education with my less fortunate brothers and sisters."

My use of the term "masses" was deliberate. I wanted to convey a specific message to the students at the university. "The masses" was a popular slogan among student activists to indicate their concern for the common people in Liberia. According to these militants, it represented their preparedness to work in "the supreme interest" of the less fortunate majority. Unfortunately, very few of these vocal advocates ever demonstrated the practical will to return to the rural areas of the country from which they came. Yet thousands of boys and girls, particularly in the rural areas, needed to be liberated from the shackles of ignorance—a common obstacle to national development. What the activists lacked was the matching of campus political slogans with existing realities.

Right after graduation, I was interviewed again, this time over ELWA, the Christian radio station in Monrovia. J. Gardea Henry was the head of the Bassa Language Program for the station. He is now a UMC pastor. Gardea posed the same question as the previous interviewer. My answer remained the same. Nothing was going to make me change my mind.

The leadership of The United Methodist Church also knew of my determination. I had committed myself to return to Camphor when I accepted the Church's scholarship. They also knew I hadn't changed my mind. In November 1977, the month before graduation, I happened to meet Bishop Bennie Warner at the UMC Central Office.

"John," the bishop asked me, "when are you going to Camphor Mission? Because I'm ready to appoint you principal of the school."

"Bishop, I'm prepared to go immediately after graduation next month," I told him.

"That's beautiful," he said in a satisfied tone. A week after my informal chat with the bishop, the necessary plans were in place for my return to Camphor.

Returning to Camphor was for me much more than a fulfillment of the contract between my people and me. There was a distinct spiritual element to my decision. Over the years I had become emotionally attached to Camphor. The dream of the founding fathers and mothers to make Camphor a fortress for the propagation of God's Word among the rural inhabitants had become my dream as well. They had wanted the light of knowledge to shine among hundreds of promising young people in the midst of mass illiteracy. So did I.

In March 1978, I moved to Camphor with my five-year-old son Trocon. (I will say more about Trocon and his brothers in the next chapter.) It was just a few days before the formal opening of school but the campus was almost deserted—the students were still away, and the Earlys were in Buchanan City for their annual vacation. Only Oldman

Solomon Willie, the watchman and caretaker for the mission, was there.

"I have returned to work," I told Oldman Willie.

"Not many university graduates would do what you have done," Willie responded happily. "God will bless you. God will prepare your way."

Trocon and I quickly unpacked our belongings and went to Buchanan City to notify the Earlys of my arrival. When I presented the letter from the LAC's Department of Education to appoint me as principal of the Mission, they were overjoyed. "We have long anticipated this day," they said, "and look forward to working with you. We praise God that you've remained faithful to your promise and that you've arrived at Camphor safely. Let's join in a prayer of thanksgiving."

When Alvin Thomas, the incumbent principal, was told of the change in administration, he wholeheartedly embraced the idea. Trocon and I returned to Camphor the next day. Oldman Willie helped to transfer our luggage to a room previously occupied by the Earlys.

After the formal opening of school, I convened a faculty meeting to let the teachers know of the change in leadership and also to propose that we work together to develop plans and strategies to make our teaching more effective. "God has called each of us to faithfully and lovingly serve the children who are our future leaders," I told them. "No one person alone can perform the task of preparing them. We need each other to accomplish this task. Let us prepare to work together so that we can give the children the education they deserve."

Then I outlined a number of qualities we needed to realize our objectives. As faculty members added their ideas, the result was that we created a vivid picture of what we wanted in the educational process at Camphor. We should be qualified, punctual, and honest. We should live with integrity and dedication to duty and with respect for each student. We needed to develop a cordial relationship among all of us involved in the educational process: parents, students, teachers, and principal. We should work together to help the students develop a good relationship with the church. We needed to live together with love, respect, acceptance, and accountability.

To underscore my sincere commitment to these guidelines, I told the Reverend and Mrs. Early to personally reprimand me, or even recommend to the Church's Department of Education my censure or dismissal if there was any willful breach of these rules or any immoral behavior on my part. As a Christian institution, Camphor had to reflect Christian virtues through the leadership of the faculty and staff. The students would follow our good examples.

At the close of this meeting the school's leadership was restructured. The Reverend G. Solomon Gueh was appointed vice principal and Bible teacher. The Reverend Gueh received his diploma from the Gbarnga School of Theology, an ecumenical institution run by the Lutheran and United Methodist Churches. He had been assigned to the St. John River District Conference as evangelist and was already living on campus. In subsequent years, the Reverend Gueh was appointed pastor of Whitfield Memorial UMC and later became district superintendent. In the years that he served the school and the church, he demonstrated a strong pastoral leadership and helped to uplift the academic, spiritual, and social life of the students. Alvin Thomas, the former principal, continued his teaching responsibilities and became advisor to the faculty. Mrs. Annie Early was made business manager, and Samuel Peterson was named registrar.

Just before our faculty meeting we had enrolled 160 students. About half of them came from Monrovia, several from the J. J. Powell UMC, the church I was affiliated with during my university days. The pastor of the church, the Reverend James D. Karblee, played a major role in recruiting students and became president of our Parent Teacher

Association. The rest of our students came not only from the towns and villages of Grand Bassa County but also from other parts of Liberia.

Before classes could begin, however, we decided that the campus needed a massive facelift. Everyone—administration, faculty, students—became involved in the cleanup. The girls cooked while the men and boys cleared the grounds, hoed, and painted the buildings. We all worked together joyfully and enthusiastically, and during the cleanup campaign we ate our meals together.

While we were in the midst of the cleanup, Mrs. Ann Carmichael, wife of the former general manager of Firestone Rubber Plantation, arrived at the campus on one of her routine trips to help with the Camphor Clinic. The Camphor Clinic had been started in the early 1960s with the help of Firestone and of missionary doctors from Monrovia. Mrs. Carmichael always brought drugs and nutrients for the mothers and babies who came to the clinic from near and far. The changes she saw on the campus amazed her. When she asked Ben Zeon, the nurse in charge of the clinic, about it, he told her, "We have a young graduate from the University of Liberia who's been assigned here as the new principal. His name is John Innis and he is the cause of the changes you see."

Mrs. Carmichael insisted on seeing me, and Ben accompanied her to my office. There she expressed her satisfaction at seeing the campus looking so beautiful. "Keep up the good work," she urged. After I had thanked her for her kind words and for her long-standing assistance to the clinic, I asked her if she would serve as guest speaker at our year-end program the coming December. She graciously accepted the invitation.

I should mention that the national Ministry of Health had assigned Ben Zeon, a very fine nurse, to the Camphor Clinic. He was committed to the work of the clinic, worked hard, and treated his patients with love, educating them on the importance of health care.

Classes began the day after we finished the cleanup campaign. There were five teachers: the Reverend G. Solomon Gueh, Alvin Thomas, Mrs. Thomas, Simon Peterson, and myself. Our classes went from kindergarten through the sixth grade, and the students' ages ranged from seven to eighteen. Some came for their first schooling at age thirteen. We encouraged the students to form their own corps of leaders who were to work along with the administration and faculty for the benefit of all. They elected Nathaniel Zehyu as student president. He was a popular and smart sixth-grader.

A lot was achieved through student leadership. The students organized special study classes to help each other excel in their lessons. Each class worked to present individual gifts to the school at the close of each school year—gifts such as soccer balls, volleyballs, wall clocks, Bibles, and a national flag. The student leaders learned how to motivate other students.

The initial facelift project marked the beginning of a series of improvements. The second semester of 1978 saw an increased enrollment of boys, so much so that the boys' dorm was not able to accommodate the influx. We needed a new dorm. A groundbreaking program was organized, spearheaded by Bishop Bennie D. Warner. Mrs. Carmichael was one of the attendees and contributed U.S. $200. The building was completed that same semester, in September. Bishop Warner dedicated it and Mrs. Carmichael cut the ribbon. The Honorable Charles Williams, superintendent of Grand Bassa County, also attended the ceremony.

By the end of the 1978 academic year, all the sixth graders had passed the national exam. Mrs. Carmichael honored her promise to be guest speaker at the graduation program. Shortly before her permanent departure for the United States, she donated U.S. $2,000 to the school through Bishop Warner's office.

The school was now winning a good reputation and attracting the attention of parents and guardians far and near. Many young people were fascinated by the positive information about Camphor Mission. We also raised the school's status to include the junior high level. (Our first junior high school graduation took place in December 1981.) As a result, the enrollment was much higher in 1979, this time with an increase in the number of girls. So our second building project became a girls' dorm. It, too, was completed and occupied in the same school year. Another memorable event that year was the arrival of a pickup truck donated through the bishop's office. Its license plate number, PP-32, soon became its official student name.

More students meant more faculty and staff. In 1979, we took on several more teachers—William Horace, Augustus Williams, Mark Ellis, Augustus Wiles, and Edward Philips—plus a matron, Annie Page. Edward Philips, who taught agriculture, also managed the school's gardens and farms. More faculty meant that we would need more housing in the coming year.

After the close of the school year in December 1979, I decided to spend some time with my brother James who was a superintendent at the B. F. Goodrich Rubber Plantation west of Monrovia. One night we were relaxing in his living room, reflecting on how God had blessed us over the years by providing us with a sound education through our parents, the church, and other people and institutions. There was a knock on the door, and we found Cousin John Mason Kayfoain standing there.

"What's the problem, John?" James asked.

"Has something gone wrong at home?" I questioned.

"No, nothing that strange has happened," Cousin John said. "I only came to tell you that your father is not too well. He wants to see you."

We immediately got into James's car and drove through to Buchanan City, arriving about 2:00 A.M. At the hospital, we found not only our brothers, sisters, uncles, aunts, and cousins all in tears, but also hundreds of friends and Christian brothers and sisters, many of them from the St.

John River District of the UMC. Cousin John had been unable to tell us that our father was dead! Dad had passed out in our village, Morblee, and was rushed to the hospital in Buchanan City for treatment. The doctor at the hospital had tried to save his life, but it was too late.

James and I wept bitterly. We had pledged to give him our love and care because he had labored for our education. He had enjoyed some of our loving care—we had been sending money and food supplies—but we had anticipated doing more for him.

Dad died in late December 1979. He was buried in January 1980 at Camphor Mission. The St. John River District Conference that he had served so faithfully as secretary made substantial contributions toward his funeral and burial services. The Reverend Paul M. Bropleh, pastor of the Grand Bassa District Conference, knew Dad well and gave the funeral discourse. All the churches within the District were in full attendance, and people came from all over Grand Bassa, Rivercess, and Montserrado Counties. One of the many tributes given at the service read, "Philip was a dedicated District Secretary. He was never a proud man. He was friendly and down to earth. We will miss Philip."

The school year in 1980 was interrupted in April for about a week by the military coup in which some junior officers in the country's armed forces assassinated President William R. Tolbert. Samuel Doe, a member of the Krahn tribe and a master sergeant in the army, was the leader of the coup and became the head of state—the first who did not come from the original settler group. He was also chairman of the People's Redemption Council, a military junta set up right after the coup.

When the political turmoil subsided somewhat, we embarked on our third building project—the construction of living quarters for the teachers. That year we also broke ground for a bigger boys' dorm with Bishop Arthur F. Kulah presiding at the ceremony.[1] We weren't able to complete the larger dorm, however, until 1985, when a work team from the Painesville District of the East Ohio Conference, headed by the Reverend Deane Williams, came out to Liberia to help us.[2] The Reverend Williams had visited Camphor in 1984 to assess the site for the dorm. Charles Muelheisn, part of the Painesville team, created the architectural design for the building.

To work with the overseas team in 1985, we put together a local team of twenty-two men, headed by Youjay Walter and Lafayette Vambrown. Our students—mainly the older boys—also worked on the project, led by Gaye Jabin and Edward Bedell. The United Methodist Women of the District, led by Annie Page, Esther Innis Gaye, and Annie Gartayn, prepared the food for the foreign visitors. All of us found working together a wonderful experience. When the dorm was finished in July that year, the Reverend Shepherd Harkness, District Superintendent of the Painesville District in Ohio, came to Liberia for the dedication.

Our connection with the East Ohio Conference continued for many years. Dr. William M. LeSuer, a member of the team, made with his wife Alene an annual contribution of U.S. $1,000 to Camphor School until his death in 1999. His congregation, East Shore UMC in Euclid, Ohio, invested in the Camphor agriculture project. Two other members of the team, the Reverend Richard Yaussy and his wife Erma, sponsored one of our teachers, Arthur Neor, at the University of Liberia for three years. Unfortunately, Arthur's education was interrupted by the civil war. Mr. Joe Davis, another team member from Pepper Pike, Ohio, spearheaded the formation of a sister relationship between his local church, Garfield Memorial UMC, pastored by Dr. Larry Kline, and Camphor Memorial UMC. In 1990 Camphor UMC received a wonderful donation of $10,000 from Garfield UMC. With the gift, the church was able to install new doors and windows, recast the floors, and build a new pulpit.[3] A video of the reconstruction process and a full accounting of the moneys spent was submitted to our sister church.

Garfield UMC also gave money to meet some of the financial needs of the school, and has continued its support to the present time. Individual members also were faithful in their financial assistance. In 1992, I was able to visit Garfield UMC in Pepper Pike and thank them in person for their support over the years.

We started more building projects toward the end of my first tenure as principal at Camphor. One was a dining hall built as an annex to the girls' dorm. Another was a new clinic building. The J. J. Roberts Educational Foundation of Liberia, whose chairman was Aaron Milton, donated funds. The St. John River District not only gave us financial support, but also provided spiritual and moral support and encouragement, as did parents, friends, and alumni of the school.

There were also tough times during 1978 to 1984 at Camphor Mission, because of the unrest in the country. At times, we had no money to feed the boarding students, which we were expected to do. The majority of the students came from very poor villages and had no way of feeding themselves, yet we could not deny them their education. Tuition and other fees were not always enough to meet all our needs. We organized fund-raising projects, but still we were short. So teachers and support staff sometimes did not receive salaries for months. I found it embarrassing not to be able to pay salaries on a regular basis, and disturbing not to be able to meet my own family's needs.

But God, who never fails, was always there to help when we did not expect it. One morning during summer vacation I woke with the knowledge that I had not even one penny to purchase food for my own family that day. But that morning a friend and brother in Christ, the Reverend Dr. Nathan D. Junius, came to visit me from Gorblee, about thirty miles north of Camphor Mission, where he was a public school teacher.

"John," he said, "it's been quite some time since I've seen you. I've been thinking about you and decided to come and visit you today."

"I'm glad you're here," I told him. "Thanks for coming."

I suspect that Nathan observed that things were not so good for us, perhaps even that we were hungry. After a short visit he decided to return to Gorblee, but as he was leaving, he reached into his pocket and gave me a ten-dollar bill. That was like receiving a hundred dollars! I was dumbfounded. "Thanks a lot, Nathan," I finally managed to say. "You've made our day. I'll always remember you for what you've done for us." After Nathan left, I sent Moses Lewis, the young man who worked for me in my house, to Buchanan to buy some foodstuff.

I should say something about Moses. He was a conscientious student and a faithful and honest worker who was always pleasant. Working in my home, he became like a big brother to my children. When he graduated from the ninth grade, my wife and I helped him to attend the SDA high school in Buchanan, after which he returned to Camphor to work and is still there. We cherish his commitment to his alma mater.

The year of the bloody military coup, 1980, was a difficult time both for getting enough food and for paying salaries regularly. Early one afternoon, when we had no food left for the children, I decided to go to Buchanan City to talk to some friends about helping me to get a one hundred pound bag of rice. When I got there, instead of going to friends, I decided to approach a Mandingo businessman who was a rice dealer.[4] He had just received a truckload of rice from Monrovia!

"Could you help me by letting me have five bags of rice on credit for my hungry students?" I asked him

"I'm sorry, I can't help you," he told me curtly. "I don't know you, either."

"Please help me, friend," I pleaded. "I will pay for the rice in two weeks."

I was acting on pure faith—I didn't have the slightest idea where the money would come from. I was "trying my luck," the ordinary Liberian would have said. But no matter how much I pleaded, the man would not change his mind and became annoyed. "I won't do it!" he said tersely.

But as I walked away from his business, disappointed and dejected, something strange happened. The man sent someone to call me back. I hesitated, thinking that he wouldn't have anything good to say to me. Finally, though, I followed the messenger back to the merchant.

"God has told me to give you the five bags of rice," the merchant now told me. "You can pay me back any time you have the money."

"Thank you, sir," I responded, awed and deeply grateful at the miracle of his change of heart. "May the God who spoke to you bless you."

I drove back to Camphor filled with joy and gratitude to God. There, students, teachers, and staff shared in the rejoicing.

Two days later I went back to Buchanan City to go to the post office. There I found several letters, but one especially caught my eye. It was from St. Paul's UMC in Wilmington, Delaware. When I opened it, I found a check for $3,000! It was accompanied by a beautiful letter from Mrs. Elizabeth Hopkins that said, among other things, that the gift was from the church "to help the school meet some of its urgent financial needs."

"God is good to us!" I exclaimed.

That very day I cashed the check and paid the businessman, who was impressed by the unexpected payment. "I wasn't expecting it so quickly. You're a man of your word," he told me. Perhaps he didn't remember his own revelation two days before. The very God whom he said had moved him to trust me and to give me the rice was the same God who made the surprise payment possible.

"What shall I render unto the Lord for all of his benefits toward me?" the Psalmist asked (116:12 KJV). A total dependence on God, especially during difficult times, makes a difference. God's goodness through the generosity of Nathan, St. Paul's UMC, and others was made very real to us. I should also say that the $3,000 check was not the only assistance we received from St. Paul's church. They also sponsored one of our students, Gaye Jabin, from the seventh through the ninth grades.

During these difficult times the faculty and staff were very supportive, especially the Reverend Samuel B. Kaykay who was our vice principal during 1981 and 1982, and also served as pastor of Camphor UMC. As a faithful and committed Christian worker, he respected and loved his parishioners and made a great difference in their lives. He taught Bible in the school, and was also the coach for soccer, a sport he loved. Under his leadership, the school won several soccer matches. He was later appointed pastor of the J. J. Powell UMC in Monrovia, and then served as district superintendent of the Monrovia District Conference. When he died in 1994, we were shocked, because he was still in his prime.

Even in the unrest in the early 1980s, we continued to have visits from groups of overseas Christians who were interested in the work of Camphor Mission, in addition to the work teams who helped us with our building projects. The interest and support of these visitors was a great encouragement to us. In 1982, a group of United States missionaries visited us and asked for a guided tour. One of the guests, Gretta Moffat from Tucson, Arizona, commented how impressed she was by the level of work carried out at Camphor. After the tour, Gretta pulled me aside. "John, you are going to be the next bishop of The United Methodist Church in Liberia," she bluntly declared.

I was astonished. "How is that possible when I don't have the requisite education and training?"

"You wait and see," she replied.

After her visit, I thought no more of her prediction. I was focused on my work as the principal of Camphor School.

But remembering my grandmother's words to me when I left her home, I knew I needed further education. I planned to get my master's degree in educational administration. As far as the church was concerned, I was just an active layperson working happily with the leaders of my district, especially under the direction of our district superintendent the Reverend Solomon Gueh.

Perhaps the Reverend Gueh thought I would be a good preacher, because in 1984 he appointed me a lay preacher. Then in August 1985, I was awarded a Crusade Scholarship to further my education at the Saint Paul School of Theology in Kansas City, Missouri. I had served Camphor in this second tenure through good and difficult years, and seen it grow and become an even greater force for good.[5]

Notes

1. Bishop Kulah replaced Bishop Warner, who held the positions of bishop and vice president of Liberia in the years prior to the coup. He was in the United States attending the General Conference in Indianapolis when Doe attacked and killed President Tolbert. He did not return to Liberia.

2. On the team, besides the Reverend Williams, were his wife Ruth, Joe Davis, the Reverend William Neil, Dave and Norma Perry, the Reverend Richard Yaussy and his wife Erma, Richard Nieswander, Dr. William M. LeSuer, Roland and Carol Gill, Ms. Marjorie Fuller, the Reverend Jack Schierloh, William T. Eville.

3. The Camphor renovation committee consisted of Matthew Johnson, Nathaniel K. Innis, Sarah Glay, Sarah Johnson, Mary Freeman, Sarah Ellis, Augustus William, and Edward Philips.

4. Mandingos are one of the ethnic groups in Liberia, and are predominantly Muslim.

5. Because the Camphor School records were destroyed during the civil war, I want to include the roster of administration and faculty as well as the ninth grade students for these years. They are listed in appendix 4.

Chapter Nine

FAMILY MAN

"Who can find a virtuous woman?" asks Lemuel in Proverbs 31:10 (KJV). And before he goes on to describe such a woman, he makes this extraordinary statement: "Her price is far above rubies."

I had always dreamed of finding a loving and caring life partner who would share my personal outlook on life. But as a young man just emerging from adolescence, I made some mistakes. Four sons, Youjay, Trocon, Garmonyu, and Genca, were born before it became apparent that I had not found my right partner.

The day I met my wife Irene was one of the happiest days of my life. That day I was driving from Camphor Mission to Buchanan City to do some shopping for the boarders, when I decided to get some refreshment at a store on the outskirts of the city owned by my friend, Roland Greaves. There I found a new salesperson behind the counter, an attractive young woman. She was light skinned, about 5 feet, 4 inches tall, with rosy cheeks, dark eyes, a pink lower lip, and a pleasant expression on her face.

I stood still for a moment, staring at her. Then I went up to the counter, reached out and gently placed my right palm within hers—a traditional means of greeting. "I am John Innis," I said, "son of Mr. Philip D. Innis."

"I know your father very well," she politely replied, adding, "he is well known by my parents."

It flashed across my mind that this charming young lady resembled someone I knew. "Are you the daughter of Mr. Zeon?" I asked.

"Yes," she said. "I am Irene Zeon."

Her reply made up my mind because the moment I entered the shop and saw Irene, I fell instantly in love with her. Whether or not there is such a thing as "love at first sight"—and truthfully, I find it hard to believe that there really is such a thing—I do know that my mind was made up. Deep down in my heart, I knew that I had finally found my real life companion. It was not only Irene's attractive looks that drew me to her. It was another side of her that mattered more. Her pleasant demeanor and gracious attitude told me that she was the kind of woman I had been longing for. And more than that, I knew Irene's parents well. They were very nice folk.

Almost without thinking I found myself saying, "Well, I—I—let me tell you something. I really love you." And then, not wanting no for an answer, I quickly added, "I don't merely love you. I want you to be my wife. I want to actually marry you."

Irene's response was reassuring. "If you discuss this with my cousin with whom I'm living," she told me politely, "and get her approval, it will be okay with me."

Her reference to her cousin further revealed the true nature of her character. Given the prevailing attitude of rampant disrespect among young people at the time, another girl her age might have preferred to decide for herself about marriage. The popular slogan was "My ma and pa can't decide for me because this is a New Age." But Irene had decided to remain a traditionalist in the matter of courtship and marriage. In the guidelines set forth by our forefathers, a man's intention for a wife-to-be was channeled directly through the parents, usually the mother or a female family person. A silver coin was presented, signifying purity of heart and good intentions. The declaration of intent and the token were then passed on to the young woman. Her acceptance of the token indicated her consent, nonacceptance of the token, her refusal.

Knowing that this was the background of the youthful but mature salesperson, whose charming manners had made me forget the refreshment I had come to buy, and wanting an immediate and positive outcome of my proposal to her, I went straight to her cousin. Esther Greaves, the wife of Roland Greaves, was a friend of mine. When I told her about my love and intention for Irene, to my delight she responded, "I have no objection. We've known each other for a long time and I've found you to be a nice person. But," she added, "I hope that you will live up to your promise."

Assuring Esther that I would, I returned to tell Irene that her cousin had agreed. I thanked her for her graciousness and maturity that showed me she was the kind of woman I had dreamed of. And so the initial commitment was made. I promised that I would assist with her education, since she was already a student. Irene smiled a happy smile. And I too was joyful—feeling like a hero victorious in my long search for a genuine marital relationship. We exchanged more smiles and I left for downtown Buchanan City. There I hurriedly transacted my business and headed back for Camphor, stopping on the way, of course, to see Irene and reaffirm my love for her and my commitment.

Irene later told me that after I returned to Camphor she had sent a message to her parents, particularly her mother, notifying them of my proposal. Her mother, she said, received the news with much enthusiasm, because she knew my father was a nice person, and was convinced that I would take good care of her daughter. Her father, too, approved our relationship and wished us well.

Three weeks after receiving the news, Irene's mother, Kondahmi, paid a surprise visit to Camphor Mission, to see me and affirm my relationship with her daughter. She addressed me as I was usually called, "Teacher," she said. "Janjay is my only child." Irene's Bassa name, "Janjay," means *gift*. "I had her at a late childbearing age. As a result, I treasure her very much. I want you to know that I hold you in high esteem for the remarkable decision you have taken to make her your future wife. It is my prayer that God will bless both of you and cause the relationship to succeed."

"I will certainly honor my pledge," I promised Kondahmi. "One day you will see this being fulfilled—at the time of our wedding."

One of the first things I did to let her people know that I was indeed serious was to take responsibility for her needs while she was still living with her cousin Esther. She was then attending a public school about a mile away from her home and had to walk both ways. The following year, we agreed that she should move to Buchanan City to attend the W. P. L. Brumskine United Methodist School in the downtown area where Joanna Bropleh was the principal. After Brumskine, Irene enrolled in the Liberia Christian High School in Central Buchanan. I became a regular visitor at Christian High, which brought me into close contact with the students.

I became particularly close to the students in Irene's class and accepted an invitation to address the students during a regular chapel service. I encouraged them to take their education seriously because it would yield future dividends. The students popularly addressed me as "Mr. President," from a widely held view that I resembled the then incumbent Liberian President, Samuel Doe. Two of the striking resemblances, they said, were my eyeglasses and my Afro hairdo. There was even a facial resemblance!

While working on this book, I had the opportunity of meeting Zoemar Neor, a friend and classmate of Irene's at Christian High. They used to jokingly call Irene "First Lady," Zoemar told me. When I asked why, she said that they were impressed by my commitment to Irene and were convinced that I was very serious about marrying her some day. Judging from my activities in the country and the county, they had the strong feeling that I would become someone prominent. They always encouraged Irene by telling her, "Irene, you must hold fast to Mr. Innis."

While Irene was still in school, our courtship was legitimized through the exchange of traditional marital vows in the presence of our respective parents, relatives, and friends. During the next six years, our first daughter, Chenda, was born. Two years later our son John was born—a handsome baby.

On December 22, 1984, Irene and I were married by Western tradition in the Whitfield Memorial UMC in Buchanan City. Her brother, James Giah, gave Irene in marriage. My brother James was best man, and my sister, Felicia Tupee Innis, was maid of honor. Our daughter Chenda was the petal steward and Kemoh Jallah, Jr., the son of friends, was the ring bearer. Officiating at the wedding were the Reverend Dr. Frank Horton, the Reverend James D. Karblee, the Reverend G. Solomon Gueh, and the Reverend Daniel G. Gueh. It was wonderful to have the Reverend and Mrs. Early attend the wedding, as well as the Reverend G. Abba Karnga and other pastors of Buchanan City. The J. J. Powell UMC choir and The Sower Singers of the Department of Evangelism traveled all the way from, Camphor faculty and students, as well as members of the St. John River District Conference, added to the joy of the day.

As we looked back at our life together on our wedding day, Irene and I were grateful for the success of our relationship. We were grateful to each other for the perseverance and commitment we had demonstrated that made the day a reality. My in-laws thanked me for remaining true to my love for Irene and to my promise to marry her. I thanked them for approving the relationship, for helping nurture it, and for helping make our wedding a big success.

Irene and I remain grateful to God for blessing our marriage with four beautiful children—three girls, Chenda, Janjay, Blason, and a boy, Bleejay. Unfortunately, our second child and first son, John, died at the tender age of three. His death pained us and we questioned why God had allowed it to happen. Yet we could do nothing but seek God's comfort and strength. May little John's soul rest in perfect peace until that joyous day of reunion with families and loved ones.

Long before our wedding I had informed Irene about my first boys, Youjay, Trocon, Garmonyu, and Genca. She wholeheartedly accepted them as her children, they came to live with us, and we became a close-knit family.

I want to say again that the foundation of our marriage has been our faithfulness and commitment to each other. I was determined to marry Irene because of her loving, caring, and respectful character. And I was equally determined to love and care and respect her. This reciprocal pledge has remained the foundation of the gains we have been able to make in our love and companionship.

May God continue to bless our relationship so that, by our examples, our children will grow up as faithful and committed people in their lives.

Chapter Ten

LEARNING THEOLOGY AND MAKING FRIENDS

At the end of the second semester of 1985, I received a Crusade Scholarship from the General Board of Global Ministries to do graduate work at the Saint Paul School of Theology in Kansas City, Missouri. The Liberia Annual Conference recommended me for the scholarship, as did Dr. Isaac Bivens, Dr. Oswald Brossen, and Mrs. Gretta Moffat, all of whom had been guests of the Liberia Annual Conference in 1982 and had visited Camphor.

The scholarship did not provide funds for either Irene or our five-year-old daughter Chenda to travel with me, but friends and churches I had contact with in the States were willing to help. The Reverend Perry Tinklenberg and his wife Kathy, missionaries of the Christian Reformed Church in Grand Bassa County, purchased an airline ticket for Chenda, and the business office of the Liberia Annual Conference bought tickets for Irene and me.

With visas in hand, we left Liberia on August 22, 1985. Our mothers, Conwree and Kondahmi, accompanied us to the Roberts International Airport near Monrovia. Also on hand to bid us farewell were my brothers, James, Nathaniel, Dwahyuway, Roosevelt, and Jerry. Students Gabriel John and John Clinton were among those who came to say good-bye.

It took us more than twenty-four hours in transit to get to Kansas City, flying via London and New York. It was ten in the evening when we arrived at the Kansas City airport—and no one was there to meet us. They hadn't been notified of our arrival date or time. The driver of the taxi we took was very kind to us, allowing us to pay $20 instead of the $30 that the meter showed, making us feel that Americans were hospitable people.

The Saint Paul campus was virtually deserted except for two male students who kindly helped us with the luggage, led us to the Center for Renewal, and gave us the keys for our apartment in Cannon Hall. It was a well-furnished two-room apartment. After quickly taking a look around, we went to bed. It had been a long and hectic day.

When I got to my first class the next morning, I learned that I was already a week behind, since the semester had already started. After that first class, Irene, Chenda, and I were escorted to the dining hall where we were introduced to the students, faculty, and staff, including Dr. Susan Vogel, dean of students, Dr. Dale Dunlap, academic dean, Dr. Lovett Weems, president of the seminary, and Dr. William Case, who was my advisor. I was happy to see Dr. Robert D. Carey and his wife LaDonna who had served as missionaries in Liberia for many years. LaDonna was also a student, and later was ordained as a minister. The Careys helped us enroll Chenda in grade school just five blocks from the seminary.

As we tried to get settled, we were the recipients of many generous gifts from faculty, students, and church members in the area. We were given cooking utensils and dishes, and folk took us shopping to buy clothes. We were especially helped by members of Christ UMC in Independence, Missouri, where Dr. Dorothea Wolcott, a retired Saint Paul professor with a special interest in foreign students, taught a Sunday school class. The Reverend Skip Bayles, pastor of the College Heights UMC in Kansas City, and his wife, Amy, provided us with a monthly stipend of $100 up to the time I left the seminary, and the Melrose UMC also helped us financially.

When it came to my studies, I found that not only was I one week behind, but in the lectures it seemed as if I was listening to a completely strange language. Even though I was baptized at an early age and grew up in the church, attending Sunday school and learning the Bible as well as listening to sermons, words such as *Christology, eschatology,* and *soteriology* were unknown to me. I found it difficult to understand the lectures and to make any meaningful contribution in my classes. Fellow freshmen Lynnly Picow and Elizabeth Coleman saw that I needed help. They took time to explain the lessons to me and patiently encouraged me. "John, you will make it," they reassured me. Mike Pope later joined in the tutoring process, and so did Michael Coleman, a junior, who spent time with me in the library, helping make sense of the lecture notes, explaining them in more simplified ways. Mike and Michael and their families became dear friends to us. We spent several weekends with both families, and I have preached in their churches.

With the help of my friends, as well as the understanding faculty, I finally became adjusted to the classes and began to fully participate in class discussions. In addition, the first-year students organized study groups to ensure that everyone was in good academic standing. The result was that all of us finished the year successfully.

About a month after we arrived at the seminary, all recipients of Crusade Scholarships were invited to an orientation seminar in Atlanta, on the campus of the Inter-denominational Theological Center (ITC). There I met fellow Liberians Nathan Junius and his wife Elizabeth, Julius Nelson, and the Reverend Momo and Anna Kpaan who were all students at ITC. Scholars from all over the world who were studying in the United States came together for the seminar, making it a very rewarding and enriching time together.

During my second year, recipients of Crusade Scholarships had a chance to attend and participate in the Global Gathering of United Methodists in Louisville, Kentucky. And in my third year, Crusade Scholarship fellows attended a gathering in Stony Point in upstate New York.

In Louisville, I met Leonard Whitesell and Dick Flemming, important friends who provided support for Camphor after I returned to Liberia. Under Leonard's leadership, the United Methodist Women of Calvary UMC in Stuart's Draft, Virginia, bought a generator for Camphor Mission that provided our electricity until it was looted during the Liberian civil crisis. Dick, also from Virginia, was a water specialist and had brought quite a display of pumps and related accessories to the gathering. I invited him to visit Liberia so that we could use his expertise in providing safe drinking water to Camphor Mission. Dick gladly accepted and came to Liberia in 1989. The water system that he installed at Camphor was a most valuable asset. Regrettably, this system, too, was destroyed during the civil war.

By my second year at Saint Paul School of Theology, I had adjusted to the lessons and the campus environment. Not only could I understand the professors, but also I found their presentations interesting, and they themselves expert in encouraging, motivating, and relating to students. Dr. Tex Sample, for instance, was noted for matching each of his students' names with their faces after meeting them on the first day of class.

Classes were going well at school, however, we received a tremendous shock—the news of the deaths of our mothers. My mother, Conwree, and Irene's mother, Kondahmi, passed away in July 1986. We could hardly believe such devastating news. Just eleven months before they had escorted us to the airport in good health and high spirits. Now we would never see them again. Bewildered, lost, and disillusioned, Irene and I sat together and wept.

Our mothers had meant much to us, not only by giving us loving care, but also by helping raise us under God's influence and encouraging our educational pursuits. Considering ourselves in their debt for the special preparation they had given us, we had vowed to take good care of them. After we returned to Liberia, we had planned to build a beautiful house where they could spend the rest of their lives. But that was now just a dream, a painful recollection that would not soon go away.

I was prepared to leave immediately for Liberia to attend both funeral services. But my brothers called and advised me not to make the trip. "Concentrate on your studies," they told me. "Take care of your family. We will do our best here." I found it hard to understand and accept their advice. Why shouldn't I go home to help bury our mothers? But "a word to the wise is sufficient" as the saying goes, so I yielded to what my brothers said. The Saint Paul family and other Christian friends provided comfort and consolation in our sorrow and pain.

We were also relieved by the news that our dear mothers were given decent burials. Our relatives, family members, friends, and sympathizers, headed by my brothers James and Nathaniel, and Irene's brother James Giah, were instrumental in bestowing fitting last homages as well as preparing food for the guests. Two of our leading UMC brothers, the Reverend Samuel B. Kaykay and the Reverend G. Solomon Gueh, played a major part in both the funeral and burial services. The Reverend Kaykay, my mother's former pastor at Camphor Mission, preached her funeral discourse. The Reverend Gueh gave the sermon for Irene's mother. The St. John River District members were involved in both services. Other churches and leaders participated in the burial ceremonies, including the World Wide Church, headed by the Reverend Abba G. Karnga.

That same year, Irene gave birth to our second daughter at the Research Medical Center in Kansas City. We named her Janjay Kamah: Janjay is Irene's Bassa name meaning *gift* or *kindness*. "Janjay" expressed our gratitude for God's special gift to us in a foreign land and our appreciation of the blessings we had received both in Liberia and in the United States. "Kamah," my grandmother's name, expressed my appreciation for the love and care my grandmother gave me when I was under her tender care from the time I was a baby until I left her to go to school.

The Saint Paul community was exceedingly generous in welcoming Janjay into the family. We were grateful to Dr. Vogel, dean of students, who contacted United Methodist churches in the area to help us settle the hospital bill. Our student insurance did not cover the expenses, since Irene was pregnant before we were covered. Dr. Richard Burtin, a physician at the medical center where Janjay was born, provided both financial and medical assistance. He had been to Liberia on a medical team and had made a point of looking us up when he heard we were at the seminary. He and his wife Donna have become our very good friends. The Liberia Association in Kansas also helped us financially.

I should say something about the Liberia Association. Through former missionaries Dr. and Mrs. Carey, we met John Darliwon and his wife Virginia. John hails from Liberia's northern county of Nimba. Their two girls, Christina and Andria, became good friends with Chenda. Our first Thanksgiving in Kansas City we spent with John and his family. John introduced us to the Liberian community in the greater Kansas City area, where we made many good friends. I later served the Liberia Association as secretary and chaplain.

Many other people were kind to us when Janjay was born. The Careys brought Irene and the baby home from the hospital in their car and provided transportation for us when we did not have transportation of our own. Churches outside of Missouri sent us gifts as well: Saint Paul UMC in Tucson, Arizona, First UMC in Ormond Beach, Florida, and Saint Paul's UMC in Wilmington, Delaware. The Wesley Co-workers of Saint Paul UMC in Bryan, Ohio, invited us to visit them when Janjay was two months old. We very much enjoyed the four days we spent with them. In fact, the whole time we were at Saint Paul, we did not lack for caring friends and generous invitations. We experienced first-hand that, indeed, the church is a caring and loving community.

The year after our mothers died, my youngest boy, Genca, joined us from Liberia. We enrolled him at McCoy School and later he transferred to Scarrit School. We now were a family of five, two adults and three children. The Crusade Scholarship program provided a monthly stipend, but it was not enough to maintain all of us, so I looked around on campus for a job. Fortunately, I found one in the security department under Tom Drake, a good man to work with. I enjoyed working with fellow students He Moon Lee, Mike Pope, and Bryan Fink, and was grateful that Mike and Bryan made their cars available to us when we needed help. I should add that Betty Swarthout and Audry McCoy of the scholarship program kept in constant contact with us in order to learn our concerns and make sure our needs were fully met.

Our needs were also supplied through the kindness and generosity of many friends. Some we had met when they visited Liberia; others heard about us from friends in Liberia. Our friends Mark and Patricia Scheffers, Christian Reformed missionaries in Buchanan City, told Eric and Penny Sherring about our coming to Kansas City. We had become good friends with the Scheffers in Liberia. Eric was pastor of the Lane Avenue Christian Reformed Church in Kansas City, and the church not only helped to support us but also became a warm and caring place for us where we often enjoyed worshiping on Sunday evenings.

One of the blessings of attending seminary in the United States was that I was able not only to become reacquainted with friends we had met in Liberia, but also to make many new friends for the Liberia Annual Conference and especially Camphor Mission. Many United Methodist churches and conferences in and out of Missouri invited us to visit them and to speak to their members. We traveled more than one thousand miles in the Central District of the Oregon-Idaho Annual Conference at the invitation of District

Superintendent Joe Walker and his wife Beverly. The visit ended with a magnificent trip on a ski lift up to Mt. Bachelor in Bend Oregon, where the Walkers lived—my first "mountain-top experience"!

Joe had visited Liberia some years before when he was on the staff of the General Board of Global Ministries, and had met the Earlys who were in charge of Camphor Mission at that time. When he came back to the States, Joe was instrumental in raising funds for the Camphor Church that was then under construction, and his name is listed on the cornerstone of the church as a chief contributor. He continued to raise money for program development at the mission. Later, in the early days of our civil war, the Walkers rallied the support of congregations in their Conference to help the victims of the war. They were able to prepare fourteen forty-foot containers filled with relief supplies to ship to Liberia.

I also visited Wisconsin, thanks to the Reverend Antony Fanera, pastor of the Salem UMC in Fond du Lac. I preached in his church and spoke at the Wisconsin Annual Conference. Tony and his wife Lois became our good friends. Tony had headed a mission team that visited Liberia in 1982 and included a member of his church, Jane Otto. The church's youth group sponsored John Soclo, a student at Camphor Mission, for three years.

In 1988 we were guests of the 1985 work team from Ohio that had come to Liberia and spent time at Camphor. We visited the Willoughby Hill UMC, pastored by the Reverend Deane Williams. In Chagrin Falls, we met with the entire work team at the home of Mr. and Mrs. Joe Davis. In Warren, Ohio, we were guests of Charles and Peggy Muehleism, and had a chance to meet their daughters and sons-in-law. Charles was the architect who had designed the Camphor dormitory. Sadly, Peggy has since died.

Another renewed friendship was with Mrs. Elizabeth Hopkins who had visited Camphor Mission in 1982 and earlier had sent us the $3,000 check that arrived just when we needed to buy food. She invited me to visit Wilmington, Delaware, and arranged with the pastor of her church, Saint Paul's UMC, for me to serve as guest preacher.

One of the last places we visited before graduation was Des Moines, Iowa, where my dear friend in Christ, Mrs. Beverly Nolte, had arranged for me to speak in a number of area churches.

In order to prepare herself for the ministry in Liberia, Irene made use of the educational opportunities in Kansas City. She enrolled first at Pioneer Community College and then at Penn Valley Community College where she worked on her GED. To ensure that Irene's education was not interrupted at Penn Valley, we received financial help from Bishop Sheldon Ducker, whom we had met in 1983 when he attended the 150th anniversary celebration of Methodism in Liberia. He was now senior minister at High Street UMC in Muncie, Indiana. When it came time for us to return to Liberia, that church bought Irene's ticket.

In my last year at Saint Paul School of Theology, I was an intern at College Heights UMC, pastored by the Reverend Skip Bayles, who was my supervisor. The climax of my three years of hard work and study came when I wrote and successfully defended a credo, "My Theological Journey," on what I believe about the church. I received my Master of Divinity Degree on May 16, 1988. One of those in attendance was my best friend, Dr. William M. LeSeur, who flew in from Cleveland, Ohio. Bill was on the team from the Painesville District in Ohio that helped to build the boys' dorm at Camphor Mission. Mr. Knowlden Stowell was another friend who came to the graduation with his daughter Joyce. He had been my business education instructor at Bassa High during the two years he was a Peace Corps Volunteer in Liberia. Mr. Stowell was now mayor of Emmetsburg, Iowa. Before I graduated he had invited me to the city as his special guest, and had given me a truly royal welcome. He and I were interviewed on the city's radio station. I gave a lecture on Liberia at Emmetsburg Community College, and I preached at the First UMC.

So many of my friends, American and Liberian, traveled so many miles to attend the ceremony that Irene and I were amazed and very grateful for their love and encouragement and for the congratulatory wishes they expressed. My good friend "Roommate" Joseph Sagbe was one of them. He drove from Huntington, West Virginia, where he was studying at Marshall University. Nat O. Early and John Davies came from Minneapolis. Nathan Junius, James Karblee, and G. Solomon Gueh, students at Gammon Theological School, came from Atlanta, Georgia. Mrs. Musu Gueh came from Chicago bringing best wishes from herself and her husband, Daniel Gueh, a student at Garrett Evangelical Seminary in Evanston.

Our Kansas City friends were also in attendance, including many from College Heights Church and a delegation from the Liberia Association. Members of the Liberia Association also attended a worship service at College Heights Church where I was the preacher. Irene and I were able to express our gratitude to the officers and members of the church, and to the pastor and his wife, Skip and Amy Bayles, for the love and concern they had shown us during our fellowship with them. At the service, the church presented us with a check for $3,500 to begin the construction of a modern residence for the administrative staff at Camphor Mission. James Dennis, president of the Liberia Association, also expressed his thanks to the church for their generosity.

Another highlight of the graduation time was a sumptuous party hosted in my honor by Mr. and Mrs. Joseph W. Kweh. Joseph and I were students together at the University of Liberia. He had moved to the United States several years before I came to Saint Paul.

And now it was time to fly home to Liberia. But before we could do that, the whole family flew to Ormond Beach, Florida, as the guests of First UMC and Dr. Gordon Craig, the pastor. Thanks to the church, we stayed at one of the finest beach hotels and visited Disney World and the Kennedy Space Center. We were indeed grateful that we got to see these historic entertainment and scientific sites. When we were about to fly back to Kansas City, Mrs. Melvina Nagbe, widow of the late Bishop S. T. Nagbe, came to the Daytona Beach Airport to greet us and wish us God's speed. Mrs. Nagbe is on the staff at Bethune-Cookman College in Daytona Beach.

Looking back on my educational journey at Saint Paul, I could see the rewards. The meaning and essence of the church of Jesus Christ was made real to me. I learned that relationship building both inside and outside of the church is fundamental to our faith in Jesus Christ. It was out of love that God's Son, Jesus Christ, was sent to give his life for us, to bring us into relationship with God. My theological training revealed that God is a God of peace, love, and justice. God is a friend of the poor, the oppressed, the marginalized, and the brokenhearted. In Jesus Christ, God is a friend to all—to women, men, children, the elderly, the sick, and the well. My training empowered me to work faithfully with all of God's people, and to commit myself to work with them in love. Because Jesus gave his life for all, I was prepared and sent as a sincere and faithful disciple to share the good news for the whole person with all people.

I learned, too, that to be a disciple of Jesus Christ, one must be bold, stand for justice, defend the defenseless, and be an accountable servant for the people of God. I was taught to work with and among the people of God—not to lord it over them. I discovered that vision is crucial to the ministry of Jesus Christ and fundamental to leadership in the church. "Where there is no vision," says the writer of Proverbs, "the people perish" (29:18 KJV). The professors at Saint Paul encouraged us to share and communicate God's vision if we sought positive results.

The principles that I had learned were still partly intellectual. How faithful would I be in translating them into practical realities? The rest of this book will show how these principles have guided me in my work for Jesus Christ as I returned to Liberia. God has helped me and continues to be good to me in the ministry of Christ.

My journey to Saint Paul was successful because of the many fine Christians we met. The love, care, encouragement, motivation, guidance, and moral and financial support we received made a tremendous difference in our lives. And I am most especially grateful to Irene for her prayerful support, and her patient and hard work during our stay in Kansas City. Though she went through childbirth and was also attending school, she provided the needed care for the family, especially when I was traveling and coping with demanding studies.

I am grateful, too, for the spiritual leadership of Dr. Weems and the seminary professors and staff who welcomed all of us students, accepted us, and inspired us. It was no mistake for us to journey to Saint Paul. We were equipped academically, spiritually, and socially. And we are especially indebted to Bishop W. T. Handy. He encouraged me to make use of the educational opportunities that were available to me for the good of the church in Liberia.

"Most importantly," he urged me prayerfully, "you must return to your country after your graduation to share what you learned from seminary with your brothers and sisters in Liberia."

Chapter Eleven

A Time to Mourn and a Time to Build

Before we returned to Liberia, we had one more visit to make—to Germany. Back in 1982, Martin and Ulrike Boehringer were sent to Liberia from Germany as United Methodist missionaries, which was how we became friends with them. During their years of service in Liberia, they helped to provide scholarships for needy students at Camphor, and also became involved in Camphor's development initiatives. When the Reverend Gustav Kemper, a German United Methodist minister, and his son Thomas came on a visit from Germany in 1983, the Boehringers invited them to visit Camphor Mission. The Reverend Kemper made a handsome donation toward the construction of living quarters for Camphor teachers. We also met Martin's parents, Frida and Richard, as well as Ulrike's parents, Walter and Brunhilde, when they came to Liberia for a visit.

Now the Boehringers were back in Germany, and Martin was teaching high school in Weinstadt. They had invited us to visit them on our way home to Liberia. So on June 4, 1988, we flew from Kansas City to Paris, and arrived the next day at Stuttgart, where Ulrike had come to meet us. There were some anxious moments as we waited about a half hour for our documents to be checked, even though the German consulate in Chicago had issued them. Eventually we got through immigration, to Ulrike's relief, loaded our bags and ourselves into her van, and she drove us to their home in Weinstadt, not too far from Stuttgart. We had no sooner arrived than we were treated to a lavish dinner.

During the next two days we visited with the Boehringers and their children Johann, Michael, Segrid, and Heidi. It was also a joy to become reacquainted with the Boehringers' parents, who also lived in Weinstadt. Then it was time to attend the German Annual Conference, where the Mission Secretary, the Reverend Bodo Schwabe, introduced us to the bishop and the conference delegates, and we received a rousing welcome. On Sunday morning, I was guest preacher at the Weinstadt United Methodist Church, where I preached on "Friendship in Jesus," and Martin Boehringer translated for me. I reminded the congregation of the marvelous difference they had made in peoples' lives all over the world and particularly in Liberia. Their spiritual, financial, and material support for the UMC in Liberia had provided educational opportunities for many and helped to improve the health of Liberians. "Remain committed to the friendship we all have in Jesus Christ," I urged them.

The next day, Martin drove Irene and me about two hundred miles north to meet with the Reverend and Mrs. Gustav Kemper at a UMC retreat center where the Kempers had served for many years before the Reverend's recent retirement. The center also provided homes for retired pastors and other professional people who had worked for the church over the years. The Kempers greeted us heartily—in German. After lunch with them, we were taken on a guided tour of the center, and the staff expressed their appreciation for the Kempers' leadership. Before we left that afternoon, the Kempers presented us with a gift of $1,000 to help with our ministry at Camphor.

A few days later, Martin drove me in to Stuttgart to the headquarters of Bread for the World (BFW). Late in 1984 we had submitted a proposal to them, asking for an estimated $100,000 for the construction of a multipurpose building at Camphor Mission. During our stay in the United States, however, my brother Nathaniel K. Innis, who was the acting principal, had submitted a revised proposal in the amount of $144,000. The grant had been approved, but the release of the money was contingent upon our return to Liberia. The meeting with Mr. D. Marx, BFW's Africa Desk Secretary, was warm and cordial, and we finalized the arrangements regarding the release of the funds. Before we returned to Weinstadt, Martin drove me around Stuttgart for a bit of sightseeing.

We had a very pleasant ten days with the Boehringers. I even got to lecture to one of Martin's high school classes, where I found the behavior of the students impressive. Then it was time to leave. Early in the morning of June 16, Ulrike drove us to the Stuttgart Airport, where we boarded a KLM flight to Liberia via Amsterdam.

At 8:00 P.M., Liberia time, we landed at the Monrovia Airport. No family members or friends were there to meet us, because we hadn't given prior notice of our return. We were trying to arrange for a cab to drive us from the airport to Camphor Mission—a two-hour drive—when we ran into the Reverend Perry Tinklenberg who had come to the airport to meet Tim Slager, a missionary from the States who was on the same flight as we were. Tim was head of the literacy department of the Christian Extension Ministries, which Perry directed. Perry and Tim invited us to ride with them. They would take us to Camphor Mission, they said. We gratefully accepted—otherwise we probably would have either been stranded at the airport overnight or else exploited by an unreasonable cab driver.

The Camphor campus was dark and completely quiet when we arrived. As the reality of our finally coming home hit us, Irene and I could not keep quiet. We had not been able to bemoan our mothers' deaths Bassa-style, and now that long-contained grief rose up to overwhelm us. Though everyone on campus was submerged in deep slumber, we both gave way to a loud and emotional outburst of grief. Suddenly the campus came alive. People jumped out of bed, rushed outside, and joined us in the weeping and wailing for the twin losses we had suffered. Oldman Willie, the

Reverend Slehnsheh Giahquee, my sister Sayyea, teachers and their families, boarding students, our three sons Youjay, Trocon, and Garmonyu—all gathered around us, weeping with us, expressing their sympathy, offering us words of consolation.

After a few hours' sleep, Irene and I went to my mother's grave in Wilmot Town, two miles from Camphor Mission. When we returned to campus, we found that the news of our return had quickly spread and people had flocked to greet us and sympathize with us. Though we wanted to meet with all our people, we first had to complete our tour of paying homage to our beloved mothers. So a day later we went to John Dean Town, Irene's village, to greet her father and relatives and to visit the graves of her mother and her uncle, the Reverend John Dean, who had also died while we were in the United States.

Each visit to pay homage was accompanied not only by deep feelings of sorrow, but by weeping and mourning. Then all the mourners exchanged words of sympathy and consolation. At Irene's mother's grave, we entered phase two of the visit: the exchange of greetings, shaking hands, snapping fingers, hugging, and finally the salutation *"Muehn!"*—Bassa for "good morning" or "hello." Irene's father and her people were thrilled to have us back home and thanked God for our safe return.

Later on we returned to Camphor from Irene's village. While we rested for a few days, people came from far and near to greet us and welcome us home, expressing their condolences on the deaths of our mothers. During that time, we shared with our families and friends, as well as the pastors, teachers, the school, and the church, the gifts we had brought them from the States.

Then it was time to resume my position as principal of Camphor Mission. An impressive program was held for the formal turning over of the reins, when Nathaniel Innis, as acting principal, the faculty, staff, and students officially welcomed us through prayers, songs, and remarks.

Speaking on everyone's behalf, Nathaniel thanked us for our success in the United States and gave a summary of the school's status during his tenure. After receiving the keys to the principal's office from Nathaniel, I thanked him and congratulated him for his dedication to the work of Camphor Mission while we were away. And I thanked the faculty, staff, and students for their hard work and cooperation in keeping the school going successfully in our protracted absence.

Almost immediately, we began work on repairing and painting the buildings on campus. During his tenure, Nathaniel had started to build a small principal's residence, and we were able to complete it. In November we broke ground for the multipurpose building for which Bread for the World was supplying the funds. Bishop Kulah conducted the groundbreaking ceremony, and officials of the Liberia Annual Conference accompanied him. Representatives from the Bassa Christian community also attended the event, including the Reverend Abba G. Karnga of the World Wide Mission Church and the Reverend Moses Karnga of the Gospel League Church.

The very next day we began to dig for the foundation and to arrange with builders and suppliers for materials. This was going to be a large building—45 feet by 300 feet. Students, villagers, church members, and teachers took an active part in molding blocks to be used in the foundation, and we were able to pay all of them for their work.[1] We finished laying the foundation late in November.

The first week in December we held our closing exercises, and James Garjay, an alumnus of Camphor, was the guest speaker. James was among the group of students I met when I first went to Camphor Mission in the early 1950s. When he graduated from the eighth grade in 1960, he moved to Firestone to find work. James was happy to be the speaker. "This is the first time I have been honored this way," he told us. He encouraged both students and graduates to be committed to learning because "education is the gateway to success." He also encouraged parents to pay attention to the education of their children.[2]

Work on the multipurpose building continued all through 1989 and by late in the year it had risen to window level. Residents and visitors alike were happy to see the progress being made. We kept Bread for the World informed through written reports, pictures, and videocassettes, as well as an audit of the funds, and received good feedback from them. They said they would send us enough funds to furnish the building when it was completed.

We had our closing program for 1989 in December with the Reverend Perry Tinklenberg as the guest speaker. His wife Kathy and their son, Michael, and daughter, Laurel, also attended, and the Reverend Abba C. Karnga presented the certificates to the graduates. We urged them to go forward in pursuit of high academic advancement.

On December 24, 1989, civil war erupted in Liberia. At first we were not too concerned. In January 1990, before the new school year began, a work team from Lawton, Michigan, headed by the Reverend Billy Dalton, arrived to help with our construction activities.[3] But after only two weeks, the work team had to rush back to the States because we learned that the conflict was spreading fast. Fortunately, the war did not reach us until May, when rebels captured Camphor Mission. Until then, the school activities went on as usual.

During the next few years, while the civil war swirled around us, we coped as best we could, both educationally and with our construction projects. Thanks to contributions from churches and friends, we were able to complete a more spacious principal's residence by late 1992.[4] Our next project was a new health center, for which the J. J. Roberts Educational Foundation in Liberia contributed funds. The building had been finished to window level when the civil crisis struck its destructive blow at Camphor. The Camphor UMC, renamed Garfield UMC, received a gift of $10,000 from its sister church, Garfield Memorial, in Pepper Pike, Ohio, and was rebuilt. We planned a new girls' dormitory, but were unable to start on it.

During this time we expanded our agriculture program, a vital part of our ministry at Camphor. It was our practical way of responding to Jesus' command to Peter, "Feed my sheep." The program fed students, teachers, and staff. With the help of EZE, a German philanthropic organization, we raised poultry, grew swamp rice, and produced our own vegetables. The East Shore UMC also helped with the project through the efforts of Dr. William LeSeur. We submitted a financial report to EZE on the beginnings of our program, but the civil war put an end to it by not only destroying our records, but Camphor Mission itself.

Notes

1. The management team for the project consisted of David Zeon, the Reverend Esther Gray Gbah, Peter Zeon, Mrs. Martha Glay, Peter Glay, the Reverend J. C. Early, the Reverend Zuah Madah, and a few others. The contractors for the building were Nathan Yahwheh, Joseph Kpah, Peter Gborgar, and Daniel Lathrobe.
2. For the names of the graduates in 1988 and 1989, please see appendix 6.
3. The work team consisted of Duane Parker, T. W. Lane, Butch Cirino, Irene Cornisch, Bill Cornenwett, Mary Ann Veldt, Steve Butcher, and Buster Turner.
4. College Heights UMC in Kansas City, Missouri, gave $3,500; First UMC in Ormond Beach, Florida, gave $5,000; the Reverend and Mrs. Gustav Kemper in Germany gave $1,000.

Chapter Twelve

THE BEGINNING OF THE "SENSELESS WAR"

When civil war broke out on Christmas Eve, 1989, most civilians dismissed the reports of an armed incursion into Nimba County as a trivial affair. How wrong we were!

International observers, military experts, and social workers have described the Liberian internal conflict as one of the world's most atrocious, inhumane, and devastating wars. We experienced seven years of indiscriminate mass murders, brutality, and wanton pillaging and destruction by both rebels and government. More than two hundred fifty thousand people were killed. "A senseless war," we Liberians have called it.

Early in December 1989, after the graduation ceremonies, school at Camphor closed for the summer vacation, and most students left the campus. Only my family and I, together with a few students, some teachers with their families, and Oldman Solomon Willie remained on campus. We were experiencing a relaxed and peaceful vacation—until Christmas Eve.

That evening, a group of us were going over plans for the next academic year, when suddenly the Liberian national anthem interrupted the regular broadcast on the state radio station. Such an occurrence usually heralds an important happening or a major policy statement by the President. Sure enough, the voice that followed the anthem was that of President Samuel Kanyon Doe.

An armed incursion, he informed the nation, had come into Nimba County, via Butuo. (Nimba is in the north of Liberia and borders the neighboring countries of Guinea and Côte d'Ivoire.) The group was comprised of dissident Liberians led by Charles Taylor, the former director-general of the General Services Agency (GSA). But, said President Doe, everyone should remain calm, citizens and foreign residents alike, and have a merry Christmas. He would quickly bring the situation under control.

Pleased with the President's assurance we, like the rest of the country, were confident that this uprising would soon become a relic of the past. And we happily went on with our Christmas celebration on campus.

But we all, including the President himself, were lulled into a kind of blindness. The fact that he took the incursion lightly, assuring us that it would soon be contained, bolstered a kind of "pre-Flood" mentality in the Liberian population. Like the people of Noah's day who dismissed the possibility of any change in the fixed meteorological pattern of the world, so Liberians dismissed the possibility of a full-scale war in our country. We could not foresee the future—that we would be launched on a bloody power struggle, or that in less than a year President Doe would be dead, killed by the rebels. We also chose not to remember our own recent history.

In 1980, Samuel Kanyon Doe, then a master sergeant in the Armed Forces of Liberia (AFL), was one of seventeen noncommissioned officers who had instituted a bloody coup. They toppled the elected government of President William R. Tolbert, Jr., an Americo-Liberian, brutally killing the President. Doe, a member of the Krahn tribe, became chairman of the People's Redemption Council (PRC), the military junta that replaced the Tolbert government. At the same time he made himself the head of State, the first indigenous Liberian to head the country. He also assumed the title commander in chief of the army.

Another of the seventeen, Corporal Thomas Quiwonkpa, a member of the Gio tribe, had become commanding general of the AFL with the rank of brigadier general. Other Krahns, Gios, and Manos were also represented on the council, ending the control of the government by the Americo-Liberians. But in the power struggle that later ensued within the PRC, General Quiwonkpa emerged as a popular figure, much to the dismay of Doe and his people. The general was eventually expelled from the government and evicted from the Barclay Training Center military barracks where he officially resided. He reportedly left Liberia secretly.

Five years after the 1980 coup, Doe became President in a controversial election that was supposed to return the country to democratic, civilian rule. His opponent in the election was Jackson F. Doe, a member of the Mano tribe. Jackson Doe was presumed to be the winner—but never took office. Two foreign journalists, Chuck Powell and Blain Harding, who covered the polls, reported that Samuel Doe blatantly rigged the election. As one piece of evidence, they provided eyewitness accounts of ballots burned on Borlorlah Road in Kakata, a provincial city forty-five miles north of Monrovia.

Barely a month after that election, General Quiwonkpa, popularly known as the Nimba "Strong Man," returned to Liberia with troops and invaded Monrovia to try to remove Samuel Doe from power. Forces loyal to Doe squashed the invasion and Quiwonkpa was killed. Many AFL officers whom Quiwonkpa put in key positions when the invaders briefly seized the national radio station were also rounded up and killed. One renowned broadcast journalist, Charles Gbeyon, was accused by the government of collaborating with the invaders and was executed. The official (dubious) account of his death said that he resisted arrest, and in the scuffle the gun in his possession went off, killing him.

This aborted 1985 invasion widened the rift between the people of Grand Gedeh County and Nimba County. There had been trouble before Quiwonkpa's invasion, when members of the Gio and Mano tribes had carried out a raid against the Krahns in Nimba County, particularly in the LAMCO iron ore concession community of Yekepa. Charles

Julu, a Krahn and head of the LAMCO Plant Protection Force, was one of the principal targets, but he survived, and then was appointed by President Doe as Commanding General of the AFL. So he was ripe for revenge when Quiwonkpa's invasion was crushed. As a result, hundreds of Gios and Manos in Monrovia, including men, women, and children, had been slaughtered.

But that last trouble was four-year-old history. Now, at Christmas 1989, it was easier to forget it all. And in 1990, despite the fact that Liberia was under rebel attack, we resumed our regular academic activities at Camphor. The work team from Michigan came in January and registration of students began. When classes started in March, the student population had increased to 350, counting both commuters and boarders. And, as I mentioned earlier, we were continuing with the unfinished building projects.

Early in April, however, we began to sense the seriousness of the situation. News reports from the BBC, Voice of America, and local media spoke of a full-fledged *war,* with many casualties between the government's Armed Forces of Liberia (AFL) and the rebels' National Patriotic Front of Liberia (NPFL). Government troops had been sent to Nimba County to put down the rebellion. Butuo, a town in Nimba bordering Côte d'Ivoire, was their major target, because that's where the rebels entered the country. But the reports from Butuo were telling of gruesome killings and arson by government troops against *civilians.* A young fellow from Butuo who only referred to himself as Rambo, later gave his account of what happened when the government troops entered the town.

When he saw the AFL soldiers coming into the town, Rambo said he quickly picked up his little brother and ran to a nearby banana orchard where they hid unnoticed but could see what the troops were doing. He watched the soldiers bring his father out of the house into the yard where they knocked him onto the ground and then beheaded him. Then other members of his family were brought out and beheaded—his mother, a pregnant sister, and an uncle. He could also see residents of the town being shot at close range by the soldiers. As the sounds of running, crying, screaming, and the rattling of machine gun fire filled the air, the soldiers set the town on fire. That horrible spectacle ignited Rambo in a flame of hatred and revenge against the government troops. Full of grief and rage, he vowed to avenge the heartless murders of his family members and fellow townspeople. The result was that as soon as he and his little brother escaped from their hideout, he joined the rebels. That's when he assumed the nickname "Rambo."

Eyewitness accounts also spoke of other massacres of civilians and prominent citizens of Nimba County by government troops. Nine persons were shot at point blank range in a mosque in the city of Ganta—an incident that stirred up the Mandingo community all through Liberia and particularly in Ganta. When President Doe briefly visited the town to assess the military situation in Nimba, a group of Mandingo leaders reported the situation to him. They appealed to Doe to advise the national army against the wanton killing of the civilians they had taken oath to protect.

Unfortunately, similar acts of indiscriminate killings were being masterminded in Monrovia and its suburbs by state security forces, targeting Gios and Manos from Nimba, and members of the African American community. Intertribal animosity and hatred had been growing since the coup of 1980 that put Doe in power. Among those who first suffered reprisal killings were the Mayor R. Vanjah Richards of Clay Ashland City (about twenty miles northwest of Monrovia), and two of his councilmen, Butler Freeman and James E. Coleman. They were murdered in cold blood.

Another gruesome killing that added to the growing fears of insecurity in Monrovia and its environs was that of Robert Philips, who was beheaded in his home on Eleventh Street, in the Sinkor suburb. He was employed at the Public

Works Ministry, having returned not long before to Liberia from the U.S., where he had received his master's degree in engineering. In May, the *Daily Observer* newspaper published the frightening picture of three human heads—their bodies missing. The men were identified as Nimba residents of Monrovia. Thereafter the blood-spilling spree in Monrovia and its surroundings continued until President Doe was captured on September 9, 1990.

Then there was the sad story of Johnny Nah, an electrical engineer, and his pregnant wife. They were among the hundreds of unarmed and defenseless civilians who didn't make it out of the human slaughterhouse into which Monrovia was transformed. They, too, were murdered in their home. Fortunately, their son managed to escape and later told the chilling story of his parents' death. George Dweh, a workmate of his father at the Liberia Electric Company, he said, led the death squad.

Sometime in April the rebels advanced into Grand Bassa County, which shares a common border with Nimba County in the northeast. Apparently, they were heading for Buchanan City because of its strategic importance as a seaport. The news, however, didn't deter us from going on with our normal activities on campus.

Then in May, AFL troops were heavily deployed in Buchanan City because of the rebel advances. Shortly thereafter, AFL soldiers visited Camphor Mission and asked us to allow them to provide protection for the campus. I thanked them for their concern, but assured them that God would protect them and us, and advised them to remain on the main highway that went into the rural areas. They agreed to do so. Periodically they returned to make the same offer. Our response remained unchanged and their reaction remained the same.

But it did not take long for these lord protectors to show their true colors to us. Instead of providing residents along the highway with the security and protection they suggested for us at Camphor, they began a systematic campaign of harassment and intimidation against unarmed civilians. Then we heard that the AFL had massacred nearly fifty civilians in Kpuu Town, about ten miles up the highway from the Camphor junction. When the news reached us, I went out to the main road and pleaded with the AFL soldiers to protect our people instead of molesting them. The soldiers seemed to listen, but it was obvious they were not planning to change their ways. Not long after that, their number increased dramatically and their acts of violence and mayhem against the civilian population rose proportionately. As a result, people were forced to abandon their towns and communities all along the highway, and many came to Camphor Mission for refuge.

The presence of AFL soldiers on the highway also stopped the movement of vehicles. This was the only route from Buchanan City to Camphor and beyond. Instead of being a lovely and busy road, it was now a fearful and lifeless trail. Not even the usual melodies of birds or the intermittent chorus of chirping tree squirrels could be heard. The silence was ominous. It was now suicidal to attempt a journey, and that put me in a dilemma, because there was now an emergency humanitarian crisis at Camphor. Nearly four hundred civilian refugees from nearby towns and villages had come to the campus for asylum. And we still had all the students, staff, faculty members, and their families. We were running out of food and other basic necessities. I was faced with the choice of risking a trip to Buchanan City along the deserted highway or of staying safe on campus.

With each passing day the situation became more desperate. Finally I decided to drive to Buchanan before the problem exploded into a disaster. Yes, the trip involved danger, but the risk was worth taking. But when I told my wife about the decision, she said, "John, your life will be at risk."

"Honey," I replied, "we have a calling to fulfill; we must take care of God's people, especially in times of difficulty. God will protect us."

But Irene still demurred. Several more times I tried to convince her that I should make the trip, and each time she said no. But at last she agreed to my going and began to pray for God's guidance and protection for me.

Irene was not alone in expressing concern for my safety. My children, the faculty, staff, students, members of the church, and displaced people all voiced similar fears. But really I had no choice. Essential provisions were badly needed.

As God would have it, on my first attempt to reach Buchanan City the soldiers did not bother me. We exchanged greetings and they addressed me as "Reverend." From that day onward, the soldiers always permitted me to travel the road and treated me very kindly. "Rev," they said, "any time you have a problem, please let us know."

All this time, we continued to hold classes at Camphor. We were committed to working with the children, because there was no way we could transport them to their parents, particularly those who came from Monrovia. Several times parents tried to come to Camphor to get their children, but there were too many problems.

In Buchanan City, however, schools were abruptly closed because of the heavy presence of AFL soldiers. Two of our boys, Trocon and Youjay, who were sophomore and junior students at Liberia Christian High, moved back with us at Camphor. Two weeks later, when Buchanan City schools reopened, we decided that I should take the two boys back to school. Traveling in the car with us would be the Reverend Isaac C. Padmore, Mrs. Esther Philips, and Mrs. Sarah Glay.

We started out at eight in the morning and had gotten as far as Edward Dean Town (*Edway Dean Blee* in the Bassa language), when we saw a group of AFL troops coming in our direction. Their steady advance and obvious belligerent mood frightened us all.

"What should I do?" I asked the others in the car. "Should we make a quick U-turn and go back to Camphor? Or should we continue on to Buchanan City?"

"Let's go back to campus," they said.

But as I thought about it, that seemed the wrong decision. "If we turn around," I said, "the soldiers will conclude that we are their enemies. They will shoot at us, especially since there are no other cars on the road. The safest thing to do now is to pray and drive towards them."

I prayed briefly, asking God to deliver us from whatever danger faced us. And I kept driving toward the soldiers.

Then, "Hold it!" came the shouted command. The soldiers rushed to the car, forced me out and pointed the barrels of their guns at my ears and forehead. "Who are you?" they yelled angrily. "Where are you coming from?"

These were not soldiers I had seen before, so my friendly relationship with other soldiers had no significance. They were strangers and presumably dangerous. My parents and the older generation had told me that whatever the national army called itself—Liberia Frontier Force (LFF), its name when begun in the early 1900s, Liberia National Guard Brigade (LNGB), or the Armed Forces of Liberia (AFL)—the soldiers had always had a track record of willful violence against their own people. So now my only hope of survival was in God.

"I am Reverend John Innis," I answered forthrightly. "I am principal of Camphor Mission and pastor of the Garfield United Methodist Church."

"Where are you going?" they demanded. "Don't you know that the rebels are coming from your direction?"

"I'm on my way to Buchanan to buy food for my students, my coworkers, and those seeking refuge at the Mission. Yes, I know that rebels are coming in our direction, but we have nowhere to go. That's why we have decided to remain at Camphor, our home."

"Are you afraid?" they asked.

When I answered no, they wanted to know why.

"I'm not afraid for two reasons," I told them. "The first reason is that God is with us, and with you too. The second reason is that you are the national army and you have come to protect us. So I have no need to fear."

The soldiers listened. Finally they removed their guns from my head and said, "Go on your business."

With gratitude in our hearts for God's protection, we drove on to Buchanan where I told relatives and friends the story of my encounter with the soldiers. They all advised me not to return home that day for fear that the soldiers would kill me if I came in contact with them for the second time. "Who will be with those I left at the Mission?" I asked. "I must return to them because it was for their sake that I took the risk to travel here." So I concluded my shopping and made my trip back to Camphor that same day, where Irene and the others were very happy and relieved that I returned safely.

A week later, on May 16, I drove to Monrovia to get funds from the central office of the UMC, so that Camphor could keep going. Fortunately, I did not encounter any fighting. But when I got there, the treasurer told me that there was no money for Camphor. Downhearted, I left for home. Vera Woods, a member of the J. J. Powell UMC and daughter of my friend the Reverend Isaac Woods, rode back to Camphor with me. Although the Monrovia-Buchanan highway was a dangerous one, and we encountered many AFL soldiers along the way—especially around Owensgrove, one of the oldest settlements established by the African Americans—God was with us. We arrived safely in Buchanan that night. There I spent the night with my sons. After an early morning visit with the Reverend James Karblee, when we discussed the status of the war, I drove back to Camphor, arriving about 9:00 A.M.

On campus, I called all the students and teachers together. "The situation we find ourselves in is dangerous," I told them. "But let's not forget that God is with us. Don't be afraid. Let's stay calm. God will protect us." Then we temporarily suspended classes while we studied the situation.

About five hours later, Irene's uncle, Nathaniel Strong, arrived from a village north of Camphor. He had come to ask me to drive him and his family to safety in Buchanan because, according to him, the AFL soldiers were creating havoc in their area. I hesitated. I had already come from Buchanan that day, and we had experienced real problems the day before. But when Irene told me, "John, I know you're tired, but please help Uncle Nat and his family," I could not refuse. I drove them to Buchanan, and came back immediately, bringing with me Sarah Nimley, wife of Shadrick Nimley, an instructor at Camphor.

I had no sooner got back to Camphor when a police pilot jeep drove into the Mission, bringing the mother of two of our boarding students, Johnette and Agnes Elliot from Fortsville, a settlement established by the Forts, an African American family, on the Monrovia-Buchanan highway about twenty miles from Buchanan City. I had stopped to see Mrs. Elliot on my way to Monrovia, to let her know we were safe at Camphor and to try to persuade her not to remove her girls, because the students were under God's protective care. But now here she was, insisting that "I want to take my girls to Buchanan." Not being able to dissuade her, I had no choice but to allow the girls to leave with her.

The jeep had barely gotten past the junction of the Camphor road with the main highway when it ran into a rebel ambush. There was shooting, and a police officer and Johnette Elliot were killed. Mrs. Elliot and Agnes narrowly escaped death by running off the road into the surrounding bush, where they hid for the night. The next morning they found their way back to Camphor, arriving with bruised bodies and tear-filled eyes. The entire Camphor family joined in mourning the tragic death of Johnette, a beautiful, caring, serious student.

We had already gotten a hint of the trouble on the evening of the ambush. NPFL rebels, mostly boys as young as fifteen and young men, their hair plaited or shaved off, wearing jeans and T-shirts, had stormed onto the campus. They loudly and angrily accused us of harboring AFL soldiers and government police officers because, they said, a jeep had come from the direction of Camphor with armed occupants. "Where are you hiding our enemies?" they demanded, holding us at gunpoint. "If you don't produce them, we'll blow you up!"

"We are not harboring your enemies," I promised. The rebels finally calmed down, giving up the idea of blowing us up. Instead, they decided to inspect the campus. When the search turned up no suspicious evidence, some of them decided to spend the night. The next morning, still full of doubts about us, even though they could discover no deceit or betrayal on our part, most of them headed for Buchanan City. But they left a few of their soldiers to make sure the campus was enemy-free.

Not long after the Camphor incident, the rebel forces captured Buchanan City. The fall of Buchanan engendered some wild rumors in which I was featured. Charles H. Williams, senator for Grand Bassa County, disclosed one story. At a plenary session of the Liberian legislature in Monrovia, he reported that I was killed during the battle for Buchanan. The story found its way into some of the local papers in the capital. Five months later, when I made my first trip to Monrovia after the fall of Buchanan, my brother James showed me a copy of the newspaper. The news, he told me, had caused a great stir among my relations and friends and UMC members. The news even reached the United States and Germany, I later discovered, and friends there held separate memorial services for me.

When the NPFL achieved a reasonable grip on Buchanan, they embarked on a plan to evacuate civilians out of the city. Their "enemies" were still present in the city, they announced, and they wanted to face them head-on without civilian casualties. The result was a mass exodus of people from Buchanan City into rural areas. Camphor played host to more than two thousand of them. When we did not find our boys Trocon and Youjay with the first arrivals, we were worried and did not know what to do. Finally, they showed up three days later, to our great relief and rejoicing. "Papa," they explained, "it was not that easy for us to leave. We were afraid of being recruited by the rebels. We had to hide ourselves here and there."

Among the many who found refuge at Camphor were our good friends the Reverend J. Cephas Early, Sr., and his son J. Cephas Early, Jr., and family. Others included Amin Solomon, David and Joanna Caulcrick, James G. Johnson and his family, Matthew Johnson and family, the Reverend Nathan Z. Mingle and family, the Reverend David J. Glay and family, Mr. Fred Bedell and family, and Mrs. Victor David and family.

To accommodate the influx of people, we made use of all the buildings on campus, including the church. To feed them we used the produce of the school's agricultural farm supervised by Edward Philips. When the refugees arrived, we were harvesting our swamp rice and many of them helped with the harvest. To give them hope and renew their faith, we conducted morning and evening devotional services with them, assuring them that God had not abandoned them. Even the non-Christians were receptive and seemed consoled by these services.

Then came news that shattered the hope of refugees and residents. Contrary to the reason given by the rebels for urging residents to leave Buchanan—that of fighting government soldiers—the rebels had embarked on a program of rampant looting of all abandoned homes and businesses. Obviously, their "concern" for the safety of the civilian population was just a pretext to allow them free rein to pillage. They called themselves "liberators" of the Liberian people, but now they showed their real motive. Apparently they were not satisfied with the huge profits Buchanan offered as a booming iron ore gateway and economically profitable seaport city.

NPFL rebels also began to frequent Camphor Mission at this time. We soon discovered that these regular visits were not prompted only by material and financial motives—though there was some of the ironic revolutionary pillaging of the meager possessions of the oppressed they supposedly came to liberate—the visits had both cowardly and sinister motives. The rebels had really come to weed out from among the displaced those who served in Bassa County's political administration, government security personnel, or anyone suspected of being an AFL soldier.

Eventually the rebels lined up many of the people they suspected, speaking very profanely to them. If I didn't permit them to take the accused with them, they told me, it would be bad for me and Camphor. But their remarks didn't frighten me. Now was my opportunity to stand up and speak boldly on behalf of God's people. God's guidance was sufficient for us. "Fear not, I am with you," I imagined God speaking to us. Suddenly I found myself standing in the midst of the crowd as if some unseen force had lifted me. Words began to automatically flow from my mouth with bold defiance.

"Gentlemen, I would think that the goal of your revolution is to liberate us. But if that is not the case and you would like to get rid of anyone on this campus, I will give my life for that person. Now, go ahead and kill me, but leave these people alone. God has destined this place to be a refuge center, and as long as they have come here, you must let them enjoy their peace and freedom."

Silence greeted my words. For a few moments the commander of the group stood completely still, as if in deep thought. When he finally found his voice, he said rather quietly and remorsefully, "Rev, we will not trouble your people any more. I thank you for your love for them. In fact, you are qualified to be the superintendent or governor for this county." With those words he and his trigger-happy boys left the campus. Any time they visited Camphor after that, it was simply to greet us, to find out how we were doing, and to share a few jokes with us.

The displaced remained on campus for nearly two and a half weeks. But when they returned to Buchanan, they found their homes and businesses almost completely looted.

During all this time, our regular academic classes had remained suspended, but we had instituted study classes for the students who stayed with us. However, the influx of displaced persons led to the abrupt closure of even these classes. We did, however, continue with our building programs, focusing on the multipurpose building in spite of the numerous problems we encountered at the onset of the war.

The terrible news of fighting and massacres from both sides of the conflict continued to flood in on us. One was the infamous Lutheran church massacre in Monrovia. Hundreds of civilians had fled the insecurity of their homes and communities, taking refuge in the compound of St. Peter's Lutheran Church on Fourteenth Street in Sinkor. On the fateful night of August 16, 1990, a group of armed individuals stormed the compound and opened fire on the sleeping refugees, most of whom were inside the church. Nearly a thousand persons lost their lives. The lucky survivors recalled the shock of being awakened at the sound of firing, the ensuing fear and pandemonium, the stampede to find a way of escape, the mournful and helpless cries of babies and children, men and women, old and young. Some told how they survived by playing dead when their bullet-ridden neighbors fell on them, then crawled out from under the corpses after the death squads had left. Civilians who visited the church compound after the massacre told how the blood of the victims flowed out from the church onto Tubman Boulevard forty feet away.

The JFK massacre was another horrifying event. Thousands of Monrovia civilians took refuge in the John F.

Kennedy Memorial Hospital, the largest medical center in Liberia. But many of them also lost their lives at the hands of the death squads. The panic that ensued sent residents of Monrovia scattering helter-skelter in a frantic search for a safer place of refuge. You could see throngs and throngs of people on the roads. Some carried bundles of varying sizes on their heads and traveling bags on their backs. Others had babies and young children strapped to their backs. Some men carried their children on their shoulders. Others carried their sick and aged parents on their backs or in wheelbarrows.

As the bloodbath continued, President Doe finally decided to leave the country. On September 9, 1990, accompanied by armed guards, Doe left the executive mansion that had been turned into a fortress, for the port city of Freeport, hoping that the West Africa Peace Keeping Force (ECOMOG) would provide him safe passage. But he was captured by a breakaway rebel faction, the Independent National Patriotic Front of Liberia (INPFL), led by a renegade AFL soldier named Prince Y. Johnson. In the brief gun battle that ensued, seventy of Doe's men were killed, and Doe was captured after being shot in the leg. He was taken to Johnson's base in Caldwell, just outside Monrovia. There he reportedly hemorrhaged to death after being severely tortured, including having his ears cut off. Pictures of his dead body were publicly displayed.

Besides the assassination of President Doe, there were also accounts of brutal killings of civilians by General Johnson's INPFL. One was reported to have taken place in the Bong Mining Company (BMC) in lower Bong Country. The BMC was a German-run multinational company involved in iron ore mining in that part of rural Liberia, and was one of the largest employers in the country. Its electrical power plant was capable of supplying power to several countries in the West African subregion. Johnson's men killed the workers, mainly members of the Mandingo tribe, and looted the company. Some of that killing was due to revenge. Mandingoes were said to have directed AFL soldiers to the hiding place of Gios and Manos who had fled into Nimba to escape the government troops. After he and his men left for Monrovia, General Charles Taylor's NPFL occupied the area and continued the looting, so that the plant was destroyed.

A number of other executions were carried out by the INPFL in Monrovia. Fred Blay, senator from Sinoe County, Larry Bortch, a former member of the PRC (Doe's military junta), and Paul K. Williams, a high school principal, were three of those executed. These men were reportedly granted safety in the area controlled by Johnson's INPFL on the western outskirts of Monrovia. But Senator Blay was executed when he was discovered to have been secretly communicating with Doe in order to let him know the position of General Johnson. Larry Bortch was killed because he was making personal use of food entrusted to him by General Johnson for civilians.

The killing of Paul Williams was based on revenge. When Prince Johnson was a student at Well Hairston High School in Monrovia, Paul Williams was the principal. Some missionaries, taking an interest in Johnson's musical talents, awarded him a scholarship to continue his studies in the United States. But Principal Williams denied Johnson the scholarship. Johnson left the school in anger and later joined the Liberian army. A member of the Gio tribe, he later joined the NPFL when the rift developed between the people of Grand Gedeh and Nimba Counties. Those who witnessed the execution of Mr. Williams said that Johnson reminded him about the scholarship before shooting.

These last three incidents give some clues about General Prince Johnson. Strangely, citizens in the areas he controlled praised him for his kindness, straightforwardness, and discipline. It seems he executed both civilians and his own soldiers for looting, cheating, harassment, and disobedience to orders. The result was that every infrastructure and material asset remained intact in areas he commanded. His philosophy on guns and government helped boost his popularity among war-weary Liberians, particularly Monrovians. He believed that those who professed to liberate the poor and oppressed but ended up slaughtering them were not fit to lead the government that would emerge from the rebellion, and they themselves should be prosecuted. So he publicly declared that neither Taylor, nor the other warlords, nor he himself was qualified to be president in post-war Liberia, and should probably be tried for war crimes. Such sweeping utterances made many people wonder whether General Johnson was really a "normal" person!

The situation was quite different with the AFL soldiers, Charles Taylor's NPFL, and other factions that sprang up later. Civilian deaths, harassment, looting, sexual assaults, and torture were almost commonplace. Then there was the Dupont Road massacre in NPFL-controlled Paynesville City, near Monrovia. Hundreds of civilians fleeing the death squads in Monrovia were slaughtered. Another mass murder, involving several hundred people, took place a few years later in the Monweh-Tappita area deep in rural Liberia, controlled by the NPFL. Those killed were mainly from the Bassa tribe who had fled there by the thousands. Those who survived the butchery quoted the Gio and Mano perpetrators as saying that it was retaliation for a demonstration the Bassa people had staged against them in Buchanan and Monrovia in 1992. But that demonstration had called for the Gios and Manos to leave all Bassa territories because they were killing innocent people in those areas, especially in Buchanan, under the pretext that they were either government supporters or sympathizers of the AFL.

The security situation in Monrovia and the surrounding towns became more precarious when the rebels reached the city's outskirts. Prince Johnson's breakaway INPFL was the first to reach Monrovia. But there were more and more reports of massacres by NPFL troops—the Dupont Road massacre; the massacre at the Carter Camp Displaced Persons Center on the Firestone Rubber Plantation where more than one hundred persons were killed and many others wounded.

At Camphor, we managed to survive during the rest of 1990. For this we gave thanks for God's continued divine intervention. The immense contribution and sacrifices of all the dedicated and committed leaders with whom I shared the responsibility at Camphor during the war cannot be overemphasized. We operated with a team spirit that got things done for the best interests of those we had to serve. God blessed and guided us in our working relationship. Cooperation, courage, and prayers became the hallmark of our collective leadership, enabling us to forge ahead positively. Our team included Robert Early as vice principal, Samuel B. Gaye as registrar, Abraham Cooper as business manager, Edward Philip as agriculture coordinator. Our teachers were Eric Davis, Roosevelt Innis, Arthur Neor, Comfort Lloyd, Mark Ellis, John Barlinyu and Jerry Giah. In our medical program, which played such an important role during those critical times, there were Augustus William as physician's assistant, Ducan Kamara as nurse, Irene Innis as nurse assistant, and Jerry Innis as registrar of the clinic. Edith Gardner was our matron and Sayyea Innis our dietitian. Our campus custodians were Moses Lewis, Matthew Anthony, Nathaniel Whayongar, and Borbor Fineboy.

Through our clinic we were able to cater to the health needs of thousands of displaced children, women, men, and elderly. People also traveled thirty to forty miles on foot to get medical help. Crucial cases that we could not handle were referred to the LAMCO and government hospitals in Buchanan. But we would not have been able to render these valuable services had it not been for the help of Martin Boehringer and his friends in Germany. They not only sent us drugs and medical supplies, but they also shipped us a forty-foot container filled with all sorts of relief supplies, including clothing, shoes, school materials, and carpentry tools. Martin had hoped to lead a team to Camphor to work on an electrical project for the school, but the war prevented that trip from taking place. We will always be grateful to Martin and Ulrike and their church and friends who helped us meet the needs of people caught in a desperate civil conflict.

Chapter Thirteen

We Get Caught in Operation Octopus

For the last part of 1990 and through 1991, we did not hold regular classes. We did, however, conduct tutorial classes to keep the students occupied, and when the war subsided for a while we sent some of the students to join their parents in Monrovia. Early in 1992, we started regular classes again.

The unsettled political situation during these days dragged on. Prince Johnson and Charles Taylor continued to battle each other for control of the NPFL and the government. At the end of 1990, a cease-fire was called by ECOWAS, the Economic Community of West African States, which sent troops (ECOMOG) into Liberia to try to keep the peace. But fighting between factions continued, and also between the NPFL and the ECOMOG. No elections were held until 1997, but in 1991 Charles Taylor declared himself president. Taylor was not recognized by ECOWAS, however, who appointed a temporary president, Dr. Amos Sawyer.

At the end of 1991, the Annual Conference of the LAC was held in Gompa City, Nimba County. At that conference I was ordained an elder by Bishop Kulah, and then was appointed to be the pastor of the Camphor church, now called Garfield UMC. (I had been ordained deacon in 1989.) In May of 1992, I made a trip to the United States in order to be an observer at the General Conference of the UMC, which was held in Louisville, Kentucky. I was able also to visit a number of Liberian friends including Nathan Junius and Dr. Emmanuel Bailey. The Reverend Perry Tinklenberg, who had worked with the Christian Extension Ministries in Buchanan in the 1980s, invited me out to Spokane where he was now the pastor of New Hope Christian Reformed Church. I spent a pleasant four days with the Tinklenbergs and preached in the morning service that Sunday, presenting the needs of Liberia and the opportunities for service. On that trip Perry gave me my second "mountain-top" experience when we drove to the top of Mount Spokane.

In October 1992, news reached us of a heavy offensive against Monrovia launched by the NPFL. At dawn on October 15, rebel troops had made an all-front surprise attack on the West African Peace Keeping Force (ECOMOG) which was positioned on the city's outskirts, The attack was code-named "Operation Octopus," after the sea creature with deadly tentacles—describing the multifaceted attack aimed at placing a strangle hold on Monrovia and eventually establishing a military junta.

In 1992, we were wiser than we had been in 1989. We did not receive the news of Operation Octopus passively. Experience had taught us not to take war for granted. Nearly everyone on campus had family members, relations, and friends in Monrovia. Our brothers and sisters in Christ were also in Monrovia. In fact, a good number of our students had parents and guardians in Monrovia. Through our worry and concern, however, we continued to hold classes, even after all schools in Buchanan City were closed. Later we learned that many people from Buchanan had taken refuge in the Côte d'Ivoire.

At some point during the fighting, Prince Johnson managed to escape to the ECOMOG base on Bushrod Island when his Caldwell base was attacked by the NPFL. From there he was evacuated to Nigeria. By the end of 1992, ECOMOG had successfully repelled the NPFL from Monrovia and its surroundings. As the troops fled southward along the coast, the ECOMOG pursued them in order to prevent any subsequent attacks. This helped to make Monrovia the safe haven that it was for hundreds of thousands during the days that followed. But this was also the reason that Operation Octopus finally spilled over into Grand Bassa, Rivercess, Sinoe, and Maryland counties. And that is how Camphor Mission experienced the second major aftermath of the Liberian Civil War.

At the beginning of Operation Octopus, we urged our boys, Trocon and Youjay, to leave Buchanan and travel to the Côte d'Ivoire for refuge. We did not want them to be forcibly recruited into the rebel army. They were able to make it to Danané in the Côte d'Ivoire where they attended the United Methodist and Seventh Day Adventist refugee schools there. After a year the boys moved to Ghana where they attended the N'Sein secondary school near the Côte d'Ivoire border. Later we sent two of their brothers, Garmonyu and Genca, to join them.

The ferocity of the fighting between the NPFL and the ECOMOG and its allies in Monrovia created another wave of mass displacement to Camphor. The number of refugees rose astronomically from not only Monrovia, but also from the provincial towns of Kakata and Owensgrove, and from the rubber plantation in the city of Harbel. Others came from the cities of Buchanan, Greenville, Cestos, and Harper. My brother James and his family, who had been living on the outskirts of Monrovia, were among the refugees who came to Camphor. Not only was Camphor overcrowded but so were the adjoining towns and villages. We were faced with the tremendous challenge of catering to the basic needs of severely traumatized people as well as caring for the many pupils entrusted to our care. In my own home, in addition to the members of my own household, we took care of more than seventy-five people—relatives and friends who fled from Buchanan City. Aunt Popo, Annie Strong, Mrs. Julia Moore, Mr. and Mrs. Julius Aryee were a few of them.

To meet the humanitarian challenge, we worked with the Catholic Relief Service (CRS) to provide food and basic necessities for the displaced not only on the campus but also in the surrounding areas. In order to provide shelter for these people, we had to close the school to make room. The clinic staff, under the leadership of Augustus Williams, worked tirelessly to treat the ill and save lives.

In spite of the overcrowding and the challenge of meeting so many needs, we remained committed to our building projects. By now the multipurpose building was 98 percent complete—enough for us to begin holding classes there.

By April 1993, ECOMOG had taken complete control of Buchanan City, and the NPFL soldiers were forced to retreat into the rural areas, while the peacekeeping forces pursued them. The fleeing and traumatized civilians had their money and meager possessions forcibly taken away. The men who were declared "suspicious" were "duck fowl tabbed"—their hands were tied tightly behind their backs in such a way that their chests protruded forward, making them look like ducks. Many still carry the scars of the duck fowl tabbing on their arms today. The women had their genitals searched to make sure they were not concealing grenades and other lethal explosives. In another form of torture, plastic bags were set on fire, and the droplets of melting plastic allowed to drip on the naked bodies of their victims. No town, hamlet, or village throughout the country escaped rape, torture, or death.

The rebels also confiscated all the food, livestock, clothes, utensils, and other valuables of those in the rural areas. Men and boys were used as forced laborers to carry the items forcibly seized from the people. All the concession facilities throughout Liberia were massively looted. The result was that hunger became a formidable factor confronting the civilian population. Those in rural areas were able to live on bush yams and nonnutritional tubers of cassava farms that had been abandoned for five years or more. But starvation was especially felt in Monrovia where many people died from lack of food or from eating poisonous plants. The BBC's Elizabeth Blont described how Monrovians were eating "iron meat"—the meat of tiny snails found in mangrove swamps along the coast. These tiny snails are commonly called "kiss me." They have very hard funnel- or cone-shaped shells with very sharp ends containing the meat. The sharp ends are chopped off, then vigorously shaken in a small amount of water several times to get rid of the sand, mud and bitterness. After that they are boiled for about eight to ten minutes. To get the meat out of the half shell, the eater must suck it out—hence the name "kiss me." The snails are so tiny it would take several dozens to satisfy one person's hunger, especially if that's the only meal of the day, as it was for many during the war.

On April 3, Palm Sunday, while we were preparing for the morning worship service, rebels raided Camphor Mission. Almost everyone on the campus fled panic-stricken into the bush outside the mission. Confronting the rebel soldiers, I tried to stop them from doing any harm, speaking in a calm and nonviolent manner, as the spiritual leader and spokesperson for Camphor. Enraged by my attempt to stop them, a group of rebels shot at my brother James and me, then jumped on me with the ferocity of mad bulls. They beat me furiously with the butts and nozzles of their guns, inflicting severe wounds and lacerations on my head and body. I cried for help, but when James and two other refugees tried to help me, they too were beaten. The rebels also tried to find my family in the dense woods outside the mission, but God kept them safe.

Finally the rebels left. When Irene and the children came out from hiding they were overjoyed to see me alive but distressed at my severe bleeding and my wounds. She had heard my cry for help but realized there was nothing she could do, except to cry prayerfully and confidently to God for my deliverance. Thankfully, her prayer was answered. At nightfall, some of the refugees took courage and returned to Camphor. Irene helped Martha Glay and Augustus Williams put ten stitches in my head at the Camphor Clinic.

The next morning, Monday, April 4, Fred Chunchun, one of my parishioners, came running onto the campus. "Rev," he said breathlessly, "the rebels have bad plans for you! They're coming in a group and are talking about killing you. You must leave quickly."

"No," I told him, "I am not going anywhere. Let them come and kill me."

Brother Chunchun knelt at my feet. "Please," he pleaded, "please go away! We don't want you to die, because when you die it means we are all dead too!"

This passionate plea from an elderly man aroused a deep feeling of humility and obedience within me. I immediately gave in to his urging and took off into the bush, but I didn't go far. A few minutes later the rebels came onto the campus, shooting wildly into the air and shouting, "Wherever we find him, we'll kill him." When they could not find me, they broke into our house and loaded all of our belongings into our personal car, the mission's van, and a business truck my Lebanese friend, Touffic Azam, had brought over for safekeeping. They also took other stuff from the mission and drove off with the vehicles.

This time, Irene and I were together hiding in the bush along with my brother Roosevelt. When we heard the shooting and the threats, the three of us went further into the high forest and joined Conway Gartayn, a UMC pastor, in the hideout he had prepared. There we met my cousin Ruth Neor and our children along with most of the refugees from Buchanan City who had been living with us. We assured them that God would deliver us at the right time.

We had spent two nights in our forest haven when an ECOMOG representative came to our hideout. The group in Buchanan had heard that my life and the lives of thousands of displaced people were in danger, and this man had come to take us all to Buchanan. He cautiously spread the word around, and by two o'clock the next morning we left for Buchanan on foot. After four hours' walk, the multitude arrived at Hardlandsville (Big Joe Town), about five miles from Buchanan City, where we spent a couple of nights. My group and I slept in the African Methodist Episcopal Church.

When news of the attack on my life reached the United Methodist Conference Center in Monrovia, Bishop Kulah sent the Reverend Alexander Boe to Bassa to find out the facts. We were still at Hardlandsville when he arrived and discovered that the story of my death was not true. The night the Reverend Boe left, many of us could hardly sleep. There seemed to be strange movements and whisperings among the government AFL troops assigned to where we were. In fact, the soldiers had informed us that the rebels had earlier attacked their position in Big Joe Town, so they were in an angry mood and their maneuverings conveyed an ominous impression. We thought that perhaps we were being blacklisted as a mixture of NPFL rebels and their sympathizers. Fear of an impending massacre gripped us, so early the next morning we moved further down toward the coast into the compound of TIMCO, a timber company operating in Grand Bassa.

At TIMCO we learned that Dr. Amos C. Sawyer, president of the Interim Government of National Unity (IGNU), established by ECOWAS, was visiting Buchanan to see the liberated city and console its traumatized population. All displaced persons were asked to gather on the premises of the Flour Milling Company, owned and operated by a Lebanese business tycoon, Rafic Eldin. He was still in Buchanan when the NPFL captured the city. His milling plant was massively looted in the process and then became a center for the displaced.

About fifty thousand people had gathered at the flourmill when Dr. Sawyer arrived. He greeted us warmly and expressed deep sorrow for our plight and especially for the children and the elderly. His government, he said, would do everything it could to protect us and cater to the immediate needs of citizens and residents in areas of Bassa liberated by the West African Liberating Force. He urged us to cooperate with ECOMOG, which was responsible for providing security for all areas under its control, in order to facilitate the peace process. To demonstrate his love and concern for the people, Dr. Sawyer presented the assembly with a purse of ten thousand Liberian dollars.

During the proceedings a former college mate of mine, Commany Wisseh, spotted me among the crowd and greeted me cheerfully. Wisseh was a member of Dr. Sawyer's delegation. He said he would try to arrange for me to meet Dr. Sawyer, who had been my political science professor at the University of Liberia. Unfortunately, the opportunity did not arise, possibly because ECOMOG soldiers were taking no chances in this newly liberated area, and kept President Sawyer heavily guarded. But I appreciated Wisseh's making the attempt. That offer and his recognition of me made me very happy.

After Dr. Sawyer left, I contacted a Nigerian ECOMOG soldier and asked for a pass for my family and me to enter Buchanan. The Nigerian contingent conducted a thorough screening to make sure I was not a rebel. During the screening process I also pleaded with them for my friend, Pastor Conway Gartayn, who had been arrested, stripped and jailed because a captured rebel had said that Conway was one of them. Conway was not a rebel, I told them, and begged for his release, but it was to no avail. Fortunately, a few days later Conway was released. We celebrated his release with great joy, glorifying God and reminding ourselves that even in the midst of tough situations, God remains good to us. Conway's release was a perfect demonstration of God's love and care.

At the end of the screening process, we were given our pass and found our way to the Whitfield UMC parsonage in Buchanan, where we took refuge. But around midnight, a contingent of Ghanaian ECOMOG troops removed us from the parsonage and took us a few blocks away to the campus of the W. P. L. Brumskine UMC High School as part of what they termed "mopping up." The next day, though, we moved back to the Whitfield parsonage. Other displaced persons also occupied the church. Amos Nappy and his wife Marpu, members of the Whitfield church, heard about us and brought us rice, oil, charcoal, and other items.

We hadn't been in Buchanan very long when a delegation from the office of Bishop Kulah came from Monrovia to escort my family and me to that city. When the Reverend Boe returned from meeting with us at Big Joe Town, he reported my condition to the bishop's office, with the result that the bishop's administrative assistant, the Reverend John N. Punni, decided that we should be moved. The Reverend Momoh Kpaan headed the delegation of six ministers. On May 14, 1993, we left Buchanan for Monrovia to begin life again.

Chapter Fourteen

Respite in Monrovia

It was a relief to arrive safely in Monrovia where we hoped to rebuild our lives. We were taken to the modest UMC missionary compound at the beach end of Twelfth Street in Sinkor, a Monrovia suburb. The missionaries formerly living there had been recalled by the General Board of Global Missions during the early days of the war, so the compound was empty. The UMC Relief Department provided us with food, cooking utensils, and other necessities to begin life in the city. Relatives, friends, and members of the J. J. Powell UMC also provided assistance.

While we were getting settled, I was taken to St. Joseph's Catholic Hospital for medical attention. Thankfully, the medical treatment at Camphor Clinic had given me a good start on the road to healing. In the following days we registered the children—Chenda, Janjay, and Bleejay—at the J. J. Roberts Elementary and Junior High School. Blason, who was only three years old at the time, was placed in a UMW day care center. When she was old enough, she joined her sisters and brothers at the Roberts school. In 1995, Chenda graduated from ninth grade at J. J. Roberts and the following year enrolled at the College of West Africa, a UMC high school in Monrovia.

Bishop Kulah had been in the United States during these latest troubles, but he returned not long after we arrived in Monrovia. He asked me to be associate director of the Relief Department, a position I was glad to take.

In order to care for the displaced boys and girls of Camphor Mission, we began the process of establishing a school. We found a building in Teenway Town, Buchanan City, and contacted the owners, an Apostolic Pentecostal church, to ask them if they would allow us to use the building. The officials of the church willingly granted us permission, and the school was begun. John Bahdaynyu, Eric Davis, Roosevelt Innis, and Jerry Innis managed the school and were the teachers, while I provided general supervision. Eventually the enrollment increased so much that the building could not contain the influx and we had to think about building. In 1995, with the help of the Reverend David Verdier, a UMC pastor, we were able to lease three lots from the Caulcrick family in Buchanan City. The Reverend Verdier later became the school's vice principal.

The United Methodist Church in Germany and the Women's Division of the General Board of Global Ministries in the United States provided funds to erect a temporary building on the lots. Thanks to Martin Boehringer, who was now teaching at Moerike Gymnasium in Ludwigsburg, a city between Beitigheim and Stuttgart in Germany, that school also gave money for the project. I was able to visit Germany and the Boehringers early in 1995 and spoke to the students at Moerike Gymnasium about Liberia.

We began construction of the building in January 1996 and finished it in March. Bishop Kulah dedicated the building. Mr. David Cassell, an experienced teacher with a master's degree in educational psychology, was recommended to the Department of Education to head the school, and the recommendation was approved. However, due to an administrative problem, he was relieved of his post in 1998 and the Reverend Isaac C. Padmore was appointed principal. That year the school was renamed the J. Cephas Early UMC School. Most of the Camphor students, however, went back to the main campus back at Tubmanville Township.

Early in 1994, Bishop Kulah had appointed me as his administrative assistant. The assignment entailed preparing the bishop's sermons, substituting for him, and readying his itineraries for both local and foreign travel. I not only coordinated visits to the bishop's office, but also saw to it that foreign episcopal guests were well accommodated and cared for. With the bishop's approval, I embarked on a project of compiling and editing his sermons for publication, but the documents were destroyed in the April 1996 phase of the civil war.

Staff supervision was another vital component of my job. The staff included Ora Kollie, secretary to the bishop, and Stephen Blahwah, Mary Ann Johnson, Joe Madeh, and Doris Cooper. We had a cordial working relationship with one another as well as with the bishop. The bishop was appreciative of our teamwork and the initiatives we took to bring positive changes to the office. We appreciated the fact that the bishop was a nice person to work with, someone who provided us with spiritual guidance. I stayed at that job until April 1996 when I was employed and subsequently appointed by the bishop to the General Board of Global Ministries (GBGM) to work in the United States as an executive secretary.

During all this time, my family and I continued to live in the missionary compound in Sinkor. By mid-1994, with a kind of peace and stability in the country, missionaries began returning and joined us in the compound. Mrs. Wilma Dunbar and her three girls were the first to return. She was the area financial representative of the GBGM and was replaced in 1995 by Janice McLain. Dr. Frank L. Horton and his wife, Carolyn, followed. Frank was professor of preaching at the Gbarnga School of Theology and Carolyn taught home economics at the UMW training center. Later, the Reverend Herbert Zigbuo, his wife, Mary, and their three children joined us. They had been with the Ganta UM mission school in Nimba County, but later, as the war deteriorated, were relocated to Danané in Côte d'Ivoire. There they established a refugee school for thousands of students from Nimba and other parts of Liberia that was run and operated under the auspices of the Liberian Annual Conference. In January 1996, the Reverend William Daniels, his wife, Barbara, and their two children joined us. Dr.

Daniels was professor of New Testament at the Gbarnga School of Theology. For a brief while, the Reverend Anthony Dioh, his wife, Jennifer, and their three children lived on the compound. He was the director of the S. Edward Peal Counseling Center in Monrovia, a ministry funded by Operation Classroom based in Colfax, Indiana.

We had hoped for quite some time to own a home of our own. In 1988, on our return from the United States, we bought an unfinished house in Paynesville, on the outskirts of Monrovia. It wasn't until 1995 that we bought building materials and began to work seriously to get it ready to move in. But the war changed those plans in 1996. And in the meantime, the relationship among everyone on the missionary compound was excellent. We became a close family, strengthened by Bible study, evening devotions, prayers, and times of fun. Sometimes the men even cooked for the ladies and children. Some nights Bishop Kulah also joined us at the compound.

All of this time, I was still pastoring the Garfield UMC, which was meeting in Buchanan. I had an able administrative board and three diligent and devoted assistants: John Bardaynyu, Etta Gbaa, and Alfred W. Page Jr. Our team was working well.

Then came April 1996.

Chapter Fifteen

Fighting Erupts Again

For us the trouble started on Good Friday, April 5, 1996. Through the past two years there had been relative peace and stability in the country, though we were on our second Liberia National Transitional Government (LNTG-II). The LNTG-II had come into existence as a result of the third major attempt by the Economic Community of West African States (ECOWAS) and the larger international community to find a political solution to the Liberia crisis. And there were still factions wanting to take over the government.

That Friday my family and I set out from the missionary compound to drive to Buchanan City to celebrate Easter with the Garfield congregation. We would stay with the Reverend Early. As we headed into Monrovia from Sinkor, we noticed a strange sight ahead of us on Tubman Boulevard. A group of boys ranging in age from about ten to eighteen were putting roadblocks across the width of the Boulevard at Nineteenth Street. "No government officials will pass here today with their cars," we heard them saying as we drove up and were allowed to pass.

We drove on to Bishop Kulah's residence to bid him good-bye because he was traveling to the United States the next day to attend the General Conference of the UMC in Colorado. When we told him about the incident on Tubman Boulevard, the bishop responded, "I knew something like that was going to happen."

Two weeks earlier, the LNTG-II had warned residents on Tubman Boulevard in the area between Nineteenth and Twenty-fourth Streets to evacuate their homes. The government wanted a free hand to arrest General Roosevelt

Johnson,[1] the leader of a breakaway faction from the United Liberation Movement for Democracy in Liberia (ULIMO). The ULIMO was originally organized to fight the NPLF, and the organizers were said to be from the Krahn ethnic group, along with other tribal elements who remained faithful to Doe's administration and were affected by the rebel incursion. Later the ULIMO was taken over by Alhaji Kromah, following the mysterious death of its original leader, General Albert Karpeh. Johnson's faction had the acronym ULIMO-J to distinguish it from Karpeh and Kromah's faction—ULIMO-K.

"John," the bishop said, "we, the church leaders, told the government to carefully handle the situation. But because they did not listen to us, you see what's going to happen to us!"

On that note, we parted after praying for God's protection on our travels. The trip to Buchanan was uneventful. At Garfield UMC, we held the traditional Good Friday service with a good attendance, solemnly remembering our Lord's suffering and death. On Saturday, April 6, fierce fighting erupted in Monrovia, and we heard the reports from the BBC. On Easter Sunday, I preached on the theme "Dead, but Risen," using as the text Luke 24:1-13. Through the Risen Christ, our troubles, fears, and frustrations would disappear. I reminded the congregation the resurrection symbolizes a new life through positive relationship building, and that should be the bedrock for evolving a new Liberia. The climax of the service was the celebration of the Holy Eucharist, and we all left the service spiritually refreshed.

In spite of the news of fighting, my family and I decided to return to Monrovia after the Easter service. The Garfield congregation and other friends tried to persuade us to change our decision, fearing for our safety. However, we were worried about the missionaries and the rest of our family members, Aunt Meeti and Felicia, whom we had left at the compound in Sinkor, and Youjay, who was attending a youth retreat on the outskirts of Monrovia. "This is what we feel we must do," we told our friends. "If the trip proves futile, we will return to Buchanan." The congregation prayed for us before we left on Sunday afternoon.

We had driven about seventy-eight miles when we came to the Camp Schiefflin military barracks some ten miles from Monrovia. As we approached the barracks we were shot at by the soldiers and made to stop. The Nigerian ECOMOG unit assigned to the checkpoint at Camp Schiefflin told us that it was absolutely impossible for them to allow us to drive on into Monrovia. The fighting there was intense.

The depressing news hit us with the impact of a rifle shot. We'd been shocked by the BBC report of the fighting on Saturday. Now we were exceedingly fearful for the safety of our family and the missionaries so close to the fighting in the capital. We had to get back to Monrovia to be with them.

But the ECOMOG soldiers were adamant. We spent a long time trying to convince them to allow us to go on to Monrovia, to no avail. We were heartsick to realize that we had traveled more than three-quarters of the way home and could not go any further. About nine o'clock in the evening we realized there was nothing we could do but turn around and head back to Buchanan. On our way we stopped at Unification Town near the Roberts International Airport, to pick up Ruth Neor, a cousin of mine who was under our guardianship. She had been spending the Easter break there with her mother.

It was late evening when we left Unification Town. The highway was dark and lonely, except for the ECOMOG soldiers at their occasional guard posts. At 11:30 P.M. we were stopped at one of these checkpoints by a Nigerian soldier who yelled at us peremptorily, "Where are you going tonight? You can't go through this checkpoint."

When we tried to explain, he would not listen, but as he turned away he spotted the children in the backseat of the car. "Because of the children," he said in a softened tone, "we will let you go." Thanking the soldier, we drove back onto the highway, grateful that he had been sympathetic to children.

On the outskirts of Buchanan City we came to a Ghanaian ECOMOG checkpoint. There the soldiers greeted us with kind words. "Pastor," one of them said apologetically, "we're sorry that you passed us this afternoon before we got the information about the heavy fighting in Monrovia. If we had received the information earlier, we wouldn't have allowed you to go. We are sorry." As he swung the gate open for us, we thanked him for the cordial manner in which he dealt with us. Then we drove on to the Earlys' house, parked in the yard, and knocked at the door. The door flew open and the Reverend Early stood there with open arms, extremely happy and grateful to have us back safely.

When the news of our return spread around Buchanan on Monday morning, members of the Garfield congregation as well as friends came to the house to greet us. Realizing that we would have to stay in Buchanan City for a while, they began to bring us money and foodstuffs out of their meager resources, and even brought clothes for Irene. (I have listed their wonderful gifts in appendix 7.)

Later we learned that General Johnson was said to be in his 109th Street residence when the fighting started between his guards and the government troops that went to arrest him. While the fighting was going on, some of his bodyguards managed to get him to the Barclay Military Barracks by way of the beach.[2]

We stayed two and a half weeks in Buchanan before we felt free to try the trip again. Again we set out for Monrovia, confident that God would lead us through. We stopped first in Unification Town, where two of Ruth Neor's sisters, Betty and Zoe, gladly welcomed us, and we stayed for two hours. As we were driving out of town, the ECOMOG soldiers deployed in the area advised us not to drive our car to

Monrovia. "Government forces" would take it away from us, they said.

We later learned the true composition of the so-called government forces. They were a confederation of two erstwhile bitter enemies: Taylor's NPFL and Kromah's ULIMO-K. Bernard Murdock, a VOA reporter, confirmed this. Actually, the LNTG-II government had no standing army. They were fighting the loyal troops of General Johnson. The AFL was far from being restructured, but remnants of the AFL fought with the General. ECOMOG, according to the numerous peace accords in the Liberian Civil War was the de facto standing army.

But none of that really mattered now. We were only anxious to reach Monrovia. We did, however, listen to the soldiers' warning, and left the car with my cousin Joe Myer. We learned later that when the "government forces" reached Unification Town and saw the car, they demanded the keys and almost killed Joe when he couldn't produce them. Joe didn't have the keys because we took them with us.

Irene's cousin Samuel Parker drove a taxi, and he took us to Camp Schiefflin to the ECOMOG checkpoint. From there we were going to walk two miles to the Baptist seminary. At the checkpoint, an AFL soldier recognized me, called me "Reverend Innis," and introduced me to his superior officer as "a good man" because of my caring interaction with them at a checkpoint further along up the Monrovia-Buchanan Highway. The officer, pleased at the commendation, not only warned us that the remaining checkpoints on the way to the seminary were very dangerous, but also he assigned an AFL escort so we could walk through them without molestation. We were very grateful for the officer's consideration and for the protection of the escort.

Because it was already dark, we weren't able to get to Monrovia. We spent the night at Gbengba Town where some members of Ruth's family fed and lodged us. The next morning, after praying with our hosts, we walked on toward Monrovia. On the way we stopped by the home of a friend named Kawee, who knew our house. He informed us that the government forces had ransacked the house. The missionaries and our family members had been ill treated by AFL soldiers. The missionaries were trying to get to the U.S. Embassy, while our family members were on their way to the home of my cousin Cecilia on Newport Street in downtown Monrovia. Kawee and his sister, Mini Dunn, were kind enough to prepare food for us to eat.

Now that there was no home for us to return to, we had to decide where we should go. Kawee and Mini Dunn arranged for a truck to take us on the Monrovia-Kakata highway (Kakata is northeast of Monrovia), and we sought refuge at the home of Irene's uncle, Isaac Judges, and his wife, Martha, in Jacob Town, Paynesville, on the outskirts of Monrovia. Their daughter had been under our guardianship at Camphor Mission when she was a student there. They were happy to see us and welcomed us into their home. When others of our family heard that we were there, they came to visit us. My sister Felicia and Irene's Aunt Meeti brought our son Youjay with them, and Aunt Meeti joined us in staying with the Judges. Felicia and Youjay returned to their separate places of refuge. Regrettably, Aunt Meeti died in 2000 from a tragic car accident while returning to Buchanan. She was like a mother to us. She helped take very good care of our children. Her death is a blow to us and we will miss her, but she is peacefully resting with the Lord.

Our life in the places where we took refuge was a mixture of temporary relief, dullness, insecurity, and the prayerful desire for the entire nightmare to come to an end. By "temporary relief," I mean that my in-laws took very good care of us. Their homes also provided a minimum degree of safety that we could not have experienced at any displaced-persons center. Life, however, became very dull in the absence of work and any daily routine. Most of the time we could only sit for hours, staring at roaming bands of armed men and streams of civilians with bundles of personal effects going somewhere in search of a safer place. In order to overcome the boredom, I did a lot of Bible reading. We shared a lot of family conversation. The most refreshing antidote was evening and morning devotions. We asked God to guide us as to our future and to guard us from the dangerous, marauding, armed bandits and the probability of the fighting spreading even wider—constant threats that hovered over us, increasing our insecurity. And God answered our prayers.

During the week we were with the Judges, I took a risk one day and walked the three miles to Congo Town, even though the government forces were on the rampage in that whole area. The bishop's home was in Congo Town, and I wanted to greet the people who were taking care of the residence while the bishop was in the U.S. attending General Conference. So, trusting in God, I confidently walked to the compound. On the way I met heavily armed ECOMOG soldiers who were protecting Mr. Alhaji Kromah's compound that was next door to the bishop's residence. Kromah was the leader of ULIMO-K faction that had allied with General Taylor's NPFL to form the Government Forces. Either because of, or in spite of, the ECOMOG soldiers in the area, the bishop's compound was not looted. As I came up to the compound gate someone recognized me and introduced me to the soldiers as the bishop's administrative assistant. "Welcome brother," they said, and I thanked them for watching over the episcopal residence.

Brother P. Alexander Sonpon, the business manager at the UMC central office, and his family were on the compound. After we had chatted for a while, I walked on to the Sinkor district in uptown Monrovia to greet family members and friends who lived in the community of Old Road. My first stop was in the area of the James Spriggs Payne Airfield, where I wanted to see Nathaniel K. Weah, the son of Mrs. Annie Early and a former student at Camphor. But as I neared his house more than twenty well-armed

Government Forces soldiers who wanted to know what I was doing in the area stopped me. Before I could utter a word, a lady in the community recognized me and told the soldiers I was a brother to Mr. Weah.

"Oh, his house is over there," said one of the soldiers. "Let me take you over." I thankfully accepted his escort. Nat was very happy to see me, and I was glad to find them safe. On the way back to Jacob Town and the Judges' home, I stopped to take a look at the house we were building on the SDK Boulevard near the 72nd Army Barracks in Paynesville. Fortunately, the structure was intact, though all the building materials had been stolen.

We were still with the Judges when renewed fighting erupted at the ELWA Junction on the Monrovia-Robertsfield highway. Government Forces and a remnant of AFL soldiers still loyal to General Johnson were the combatants. One story was that the Government Forces attacked the AFL at their Camp Schiefflin barracks on the Robertsfield highway. The fighting was so fierce that the people on the Monrovia-Robertsfield highway abandoned their homes and sought refuge elsewhere.

Our family, too, decided to find a new place of asylum. On a Saturday morning we moved to Logan Town, a densely populated community on Bushrod Island, where Irene's sister, Messee, and her husband, Morris, gladly received us in their home. On the way, we met my nephew, James Innis, Jr., and his brother, Trocon Johnson, who were coming to see us at Paynesville! They turned around and went with us to Messee and Morris's house. There we found the Reverend David Paye, of St. Matthew UMC, who told me he'd been praying for my family and me. "I heard you were in Buchanan when this stupid war started," he explained.

One of our main concerns in the midst of all the fighting was finding a way to get Janjay out of the country, since she was an American citizen, having been born in the U.S., Irene and I had decided that if we could get U.S. permission for her evacuation, Chenda would escort her sister, since Janjay was a minor. They would fly to Kansas City and stay with John Darliwon and his family, who had agreed to welcome the girls and host them until we could leave. So later that same day, Chenda, Janjay, and I walked to Claratown, another populous Bushrod Island community, where Frederick Logan, UMC treasurer, lived. I wanted to use his telephone to call the U.S. Embassy. Frederick and his family had also been stranded in Buchanan in the first days after April 6. They were caught in an ambush as they returned to Monrovia just a few hours after we had left Buchanan. God protected them and no one was killed in the incident.

I was able to call the embassy from Frederick's house, and they advised me to bring the children there. The question then was how to get to the embassy from Claratown. Even if I had a car, it wouldn't have been safe to drive it. And to walk to the embassy was equally risky. I decided to contact the Ghanaian ECOMOG troops in the area to help me. We spent the night with the Logans, and the next morning an ECOMOG truck drove us to their headquarters at the Industrial Free Zone on Bushrod Island, where we hoped to make the necessary arrangements. But we weren't able to get any transport into Monrovia, so we went back to Logan Town.

On Sunday morning we worshiped at St. Matthew UMC with David Paye along with the pastor the Reverend Daniel Kpaan. During the service the church presented us with a gift of five hundred Liberian dollars to help us with our essential needs. Their kind gesture touched us deeply.

After the service we walked to the UM guest house in the town of Virginia. The guest house is not far from the Organization of African Unity (OAU) Conference Center. I should mention that Virginia in Liberia is named for the state of Virginia in the U.S., which was a leading center for the transatlantic slave trade. The African Americans who settled in Liberia in the early 1800s established the Liberian Virginia.

During the next week, as the bishop's administrative assistant, I called for a meeting at the guest house of available ministers and LAC staff members to figure out how the church could remain active and alive, and what we should do to provide hope to the hopeless. After our meeting, we called Bishop Kulah in the United States. As a result, some money was made available from the United Methodist Committee on Relief (UMCOR) to feed the pastors and members displaced on Bushrod Island.

Two days after we moved to the guest house, I went back to the ECOMOG base to ask again for help in getting the children to the U.S. embassy. Fortunately, a staff member from the embassy was at the base. "My young daughter, who was born in America, needs to be evacuated," I told him. "Her sister will escort her." When he learned where the children were, he immediately made his van available to bring us to the ECOMOG base. From there the girls and I were airlifted to the embassy compound to prepare their travel documents. At the embassy I met a mother, Mrs. Genevieve Divine, and her three children, who had also come to be evacuated. After the necessary paperwork, those to be evacuated boarded a U.S. military helicopter and left the grounds of the embassy.

It was a great relief to know that the girls were on their way to the U.S., after a stop in Dakar, Senegal. But now I had to get back to Irene, Bleejay, and Blason. "Could I be assisted back to the ECOMOG base?" I politely asked Consul Roger Daily. "It will be safer to find my way home from there."

The consul said there was no possibility of my being airlifted back to the military base. Instead, he contacted the embassy's chief of security to escort me outside the gate where I was taken to one of the rebel commanders with the request, "Could you please escort Reverend Innis down Waterside so that he can find his way home?"

Outside the embassy fence, I felt like the proverbial hen who battled furiously with bloodthirsty marauding hawks to rescue her chicks, but then was left to die or to negotiate dangerous trails by sheer luck. The first marauder was the rebel commander who demanded three hundred Liberian dollars before he would take me anywhere. Fortunately, Mrs. Divine gave me the money, and I did not hesitate to give the commander what he asked. But when he made no effort to take me anywhere, I politely asked for my money back—and the commander complied!

So, taking courage and anchoring my hope in God, I started walking. But at Waterside Bridge that links mainland Monrovia with Bushrod Island, I encountered a fierce battle between General Johnson's troops, who were based in downtown Monrovia, and the allied NPFL and ULIMO-K forces coming from Bushrod Island, trying to get into downtown Monrovia and dislodge Johnson's forces. There must have been about two hundred soldiers in all. As I went to cross the bridge, bullets started whizzing by me and I had to run and hide. Many people were trapped in this raging battle, but as God would have it, none of us civilians was hurt. I did see a couple of soldiers fall. When I got home and reported to Irene my experiences, she was both aghast and full of joy that I had escaped harm.

Not too many days after that, we had an unexpected visit early one morning from Mrs. Mildred Dean, the acting head of UMCOR in Monrovia. She wanted to let us know that plans were being made to evacuate us to Freetown, Sierra Leone. Her boss, Dr. George Gotsadze, had been on vacation in the former USSR state of Georgia when the fighting erupted in Monrovia. On instructions from the New York headquarters, he flew to Freetown rather than back to Monrovia, and set up a temporary UMCOR office there. And he had instructed Mrs. Dean to arrange our evacuation.

It was May 16, 1996, more than a month after the fighting erupted in Monrovia, that Irene, Bleejay, Blason, and I were airlifted by helicopter from the United Nations compound at River View, Virginia, and flown to Freetown, where Dr.

Gotsadze met us. He drove us to the Paramount Hotel, near the Sierra Leone State House, where he had arranged temporary lodging for us.

Mr. Henry Jusu, financial officer for the General Board of Global Ministries took us to the Sierra Leone Annual Conference office and introduced us to Bishop Joseph Humper, who welcomed us and prayed for our safety in Freetown. We also met Ms. Dorethea Brown who had served for more than twenty years in Liberia as a GBGM missionary, and was now working in Sierra Leone. We found that a number of folk who had been working in Monrovia for various UM agencies had taken refuge in Freetown.

We spent three days in the hotel and then moved to the Albert Academy UM guest house. Mr. Jusu made sure we had everything we needed there, providing food, clothes, and money, checking up on us regularly, and taking us to various UM churches in the city for worship. One family staying at the guest house was that of Mr. Bah, a Fulani employed as a custodian.[3] We became friends with him and his wife, and his son Sulima became a special friend of Bleejay and Blason. We stayed long enough in Freetown that the kids were beginning to be fluent in speaking Creole, the local language. Creole is a form of pidgin English, probably introduced by the African-British who founded Sierra Leone.

We were able to be in constant contact with our children at the Darliwon house in Kansas City. They were in good hands. Chenda and Janjay told us, "We're happy that we can be with this family. They're giving us care and love." John Darliwon had taken them on the campus of Saint Paul School of Theology, they told us. Dr. Susan Vogel, now vice president, had taken them to lunch in the dining hall and introduced them to the students and faculty as our children. She had told them that Janjay was born in Kansas City, while I was a student at Saint Paul. "Your dad and mom were precious to the community," she had told them.

Students at Saint Paul had taken them around the campus and even shown them the apartment where we had stayed. "The Saint Paul family was very generous to us," Chenda said, "giving us food, money, and clothes. It was exciting and we were very grateful."

Chenda and Janjay stayed with the Darliwons for two months, and then they flew to Wilmington, North Carolina, to be with Herbert and Mary Zigbuo and their three children. The Zigbuos were also living on the missionary compound in Monrovia, but had been on vacation when the April 6 crisis began. They took good care of the children, and were regularly in touch with us. We will never forget the Darliwons and the Zigbuos for these deeds of love and kindness to us and to our children. The Zigbuos and a number of other Liberians in the United States also helped us out with monetary gifts during our stay in Freetown. We remain indebted to these friends who had us in their hearts when we were in need. What a cheerful experience to have friends in the Lord!

All went well with us at the Albert Academy guest house for about a week. Then we began to encounter a water shortage. Albert Academy is at the top of a steep hill, and every morning and evening we had to go down the hill to fill the buckets and carry them back up. One morning, while we were carrying buckets up the hill, we met Bishop Bondo of the Aladura Church in Sierra Leone whose compound was opposite the guest house. After he had introduced himself, Bishop Bondo wanted to know who we were. I told him we were United Methodists, displaced from Liberia because of the fighting, and that I was a pastor and administrative assistant to our bishop. Right then Bishop Bondo called one of his attendants over and instructed him to fetch water from the well on his compound and bring it to us, for as long as we stayed at the guest house. "Come visit me in my home regularly," he told us. "Please, my brother, don't hesitate to call on me whenever you are in need."

The next day Bishop Bondo came to visit and pray with us. He invited us to his church and presented us to his congregation. This was our first experience of the elaborate worship service in an Aladura Church, and we enjoyed it. It assured us that we Christians are all serving the Lord with one mind and purpose, and demonstrated again that God is good all the time.

So many people were good to us and provided for us during the almost four months that we stayed at the guest house. Several people brought water to the compound, including Mr. Safa Kromah of the Sierra Leone Annual Conference. Daniel and Teresa Dogba also brought us water in the UMCOR truck almost every day. Dorethea Brown gave us bread and other food items almost daily.

In August Chenda flew back from the U.S. to join us in Freetown. According to U.S. immigration, she had entered the country illegally without travel documents. In order to have the charge of "illegal entry" dropped, she had to be repatriated. Chenda had just turned sixteen and had never traveled on her own outside of Liberia, so her "illegal entry" was completely unintentional. She had flown out of Dakar without the slightest intimation that she needed travel documents. At any rate, we were pleased to have her back with us.

By this time the General Board of Global Ministries was working on getting us travel documents to come to the United States. Mrs. Susan Wersan of the Board's Refugee Ministry worked on our case with attorney Ira Gollobin. They sent us our travel documents so that we could go to the U.S. embassy in Freetown to get our visas. But the consul, commonly referred to by Sierra Leoneans as "Mammie," refused to grant us visas. "The war in Monrovia is over," she told us. "The city is safe. You must go to Monrovia to get your visas." No matter how much I pled with her, showing her that our documents were genuine, she refused to listen.

We returned to the guest house downhearted, but I assured my family that God would help us get the visas. When I called Mrs. Wersan in New York, she immediately phoned Mr. Gollobin, and he phoned the consular section at the Monrovia embassy, asking them to grant us the visas because our trip to the U.S. was legal. The embassy agreed, and Mrs. Wersan called us back that same day, telling me to go immediately to Monrovia with our passports, and the visas would be issued.

The following Monday, I flew to the James Spriggs Payne Airfield, a small airstrip in the Sinkor district of Monrovia. Archibald Bernard, UMCOR's program coordinator in Liberia met me there and took me to his home where I spent two nights. Early Tuesday morning, I went to the embassy at Mahnbahn Point,[4] a beautiful area dominated by a granite peak overlooking the Atlantic Ocean. At the consular section I introduced myself and presented the passports and all supporting documents.

"We have already received information about you," Consul Roger Daily said after looking at our documents. "Come back this afternoon and you'll have your passports with the visas stamped in them." That afternoon, as I walked out of the consulate with all the processed documents in hand, I was praising God. "Lord, you are so good to me," I whispered joyfully to myself.

"Everything is beautiful," Irene said on the phone that evening when I told her the good news. I could hear the children's jubilation in the background. The next day I flew back to Freetown. When I phoned Mrs. Wersan in New York to give her the good news, she told me that I should go to the office of Ghana Airways in downtown Freetown. There I could pick up our prepaid tickets to Washington D.C. via Côte d'Ivoire and Paris. We were scheduled to leave the next morning at 10:00 A.M.

It was too late to get our tickets that day, but all of us were at the Ghana Airways office the next morning at eight o'clock, with what little luggage we had. The manager of the office put up a great fuss, refusing to let us have the tickets because, according to him, the board should have bought round-trip tickets for us. "But we are not returning to Freetown," we explained. "At least, not in the foreseeable future." We argued with him for quite a while before he reluctantly gave in and let us have the tickets.

With tickets in hand we went straight to the Lungi International Airport, escorted by Daniel Dogba and his family. But the flight to Abidjan, Côte d'Ivoire, though scheduled to take off at 10:00 A.M., was postponed. It didn't leave until 8:00 P.M.! As a result, we missed our Paris flight, which left at 9:00 P.M., and had to spend the night in Abidjan. The following day we flew Air France to Paris, and from there to Washington-Dulles, where we were met by our friends Nathan and Elizabeth Junius.

As I look back at our experiences through the civil war in Liberia, I remember terrible acts of brutality and inhumanity that could have eventually cost the lives of my family and myself. The war, which was initially regarded as insignificant, involving only three tribes, was transformed into a multidivisional tribal catastrophe that wasted thousands of innocent lives and brought untold destruction and suffering to Liberia. The concept of revenge that characterized so much of the war led to the deaths of more than 250,000 Liberians.

But I also remember individual acts of kindness and words of respect on the part of some of the combatants. The day Camphor was captured by the NPFL, one of the rebel troops said to me, "Rev, we lay in ambush along the Camphor-Buchanan highway every day. We would see you driving your vehicle back and forth along the route. 'Let us kill him,' some of my fellow soldiers kept saying. 'No,' said others. And that's how your life was spared. It was a miracle of God." I thanked that young man for the information and for his confession.

Now, looking back, I thank God again for my life. God, the Supreme Lifesaver, was responsible for my survival and the survival of my family, the students, faculty and staff of Camphor, and a multitude of displaced persons. Praise God.

Notes

1. General Roosevelt Johnson is not to be confused with Prince Johnson, who was also called General Johnson.

2. Roosevelt Johnson's forces maintained the upper hand in the fighting by controlling the whole of downtown Monrovia until the cease-fire was finally declared. He later moved from the military barracks to Camp Johnson Road. On September 18, 1998, troops of the newly elected government of President Charles Taylor stormed his Camp Johnson Road fortress in a surprise attack, trying to capture or kill him. But again he managed to escape, this time to the U.S. Embassy, where he and some of his allies were given refuge. Later General Johnson and his men were flown to Nigeria for further asylum. One of his chief advisors, however, Madison Wion, was shot and killed by government soldiers near the embassy entrance in Monrovia.

3. The Fulanis are a largely nomadic, predominantly Muslim tribe in northern Africa.

4. *Mahnbahn* is the name of a distinct group of Bassas. Mahnbahns and other ethnic groups were the original inhabitants of most of what is now Montserrado County in which Monrovia is located.

Chapter Sixteen

Living and Working in the United States

Why had we come to the United States? It was not to get away from the war. If that had been the reason, I would have left Liberia in the early days of the war. I had come to take a job, to work.

Back in January 1996, the Liberia Annual Conference welcomed two special guests at its annual meeting held in Monrovia. They were Bishop Fritz Mutti, of the Kansas area, and Dr. Kenneth R. Lutgen, head of the United Methodist Committee on Relief (UMCOR). During his visit to Liberia, Dr. Lutgen interviewed me for a position with UMCOR in the Arlington, Virginia, office, which was in charge of emergency services. The position of executive secretary for development was offered to me and I accepted it. Some time later, Bishop Kulah officially appointed me from the Liberia Conference to fill the office. Now, at the beginning of September 1996, here we were.

A day or two after our arrival, I phoned the Arlington office and talked to Lloyd Rollins, who was to be my immediate boss. "John," he told me, "have some rest after your long flight from Africa. In two or three days I'll get back to you about when you should come to the office."

Having the respite was good. In the three days that we stayed with our friends Nathan and Elizabeth Junius we were able, with their help, to find and move into a three-bedroom apartment in Arlington. After we moved, we registered the children in the Arlington school system. Chenda was in high school, Bleejay and Blason in elementary school. Janjay later joined us from the Zigbuos in North Carolina.

It was mid-September when I reported to work—and the next day was immediately whisked off to New York to the 475 Riverside office of GBGM, for orientation and a training workshop for executives and professional staff. When I got back to Arlington, I went through more training in the use of computers, thanks to Mrs. Gertrude Jones, our office manager. She also arranged for someone to come weekly from New York to improve my computer skills. All of this occurred as I began my work as executive secretary for development.

I felt good working in the United States, especially as the first Liberian and the second African directly from the continent to work with the General Board of Global Ministries. (The first African was the Reverend Zebediah Mareangapo from Zimbabwe.) My job involved several major responsibilities. (1) I was to coordinate the relief efforts of UMCOR's Special Initiative for West Africa, which were funneled through the UM Bishop of Liberia and the Liberia Annual Conference, and were for relief both inside and outside of Liberia. (2) I was charged with developing a strategy for expanding development projects in Liberia and other West African countries where The United Methodist Church is located. (3) I was to report monthly on the relief efforts and the projects. (4) I was to present the needs of West Africa to UM congregations and annual conferences, so that the Special Initiatives for West Africa would be realized. (5) When development projects were started, I was to provide training for staff and volunteers working on them.

In November, I was given a glimpse of the nature and scope of my assignment when my boss Lloyd Rollins and I traveled to Ontario to attend the annual executive meeting of International Child Care (ICC), since UMCOR is a member of the ICC board of directors. A week after returning from Canada, I flew out West to take part in the Oregon-Idaho Annual Conference in order to interpret the ministry of UMCOR to the conference members. It was good to see Joe Walker, a former district superintendent, and his wife Beverly, who had been my hosts eleven years before while I was studying at Saint Paul School of Theology. I was able not only to inform the brothers and sisters at the conference about the negative impact the Liberian Civil War was having on the people of Liberia, but also to thank them in person for their generous giving in the early days of the war. The thirteen forty-foot containers stacked with relief items that had come to Liberia from the Oregon-Idaho Conference then had alleviated suffering and fed and clothed many destitute Liberians. How grateful Liberians were to them and to Joe and Beverly Walker who had spearheaded this tremendous relief project! "Please, never give up on Liberia," I urged Bishop Ed Paup and the conference. "Thank you for your unwavering involvement in the ministry of the church in Liberia."

At the end of November, I was off again to present the needs of West Africa, this time to the Marquette District of the Detroit Annual Conference, where Ken Ward was the district superintendent. Ken and I had team-taught a class on Christian Leadership at the Gbarnga School of Theology in Liberia when he and his wife Sue were guests of the Liberia Annual Conference back in January, just nine months before. Sue taught at the J. J. Roberts UM School in Sinkor. Now I was asked to be the keynote speaker for their Learning Fair on Africa. My topic was "Peace, an Imperative for Africa: The Liberian Experience." Later, during my time in Arlington, I had a chance to evaluate a new project when I flew with Larry Powell, a UMCOR consultant, to Chukuqe, Mozambique, to assess a United Methodist Hospital.

We were only in Arlington for five months before I was transferred to Baldwin, Louisiana, to serve as interim director of the UMCOR Sager-Brown Center there. But those five months enabled me to develop new leadership skills, thanks to the UMCOR staff. We all worked well together as a team. I was also able to make good friends for Liberia among the UM pastors in the area. One was Dr. Wasena Wright, pastor of the Annandale UM Church, a good friend of Dr. Nathan Junius who was an affiliate member of the church. Nathan taught Sunday school there and exposed the congregation to the work of the United Methodist Church in Liberia. As a result, Dr. Wright visited Liberia in 1994. Through that visit, the Liberia Annual Conference became connected to the Virginia Annual Conference, and was able to raise $80,000 for the work of the church in Liberia. Dr. Wright and his wife, Pat, became our friends and were very good to our family.

Another new friend was the Reverend Blaine Bluebaugh, pastor of the Graham Road UMC in Falls Church. Thanks to them, the Liberia Annual Conference was given several manual typewriters, sewing machines, a photocopier, and other items.

During these five months we also renewed friendships. Dick Nieswander had been a member of the work team that came to Liberia and Camphor in 1985. Then in 1995 he had been part of a work team that helped to construct a second UMC guest house in Virginia, Liberia. We had several visits with Dick and his wife Ann, and were able to worship with them at the Ramsey UMC.

A number of longtime Liberian friends were living in the Washington, D.C., area, and it was good to visit with many of them on a regular basis. Joseph and Joanna Sinyon were especially close to us.

Our sudden transfer to Louisiana caught us all by surprise. Irene had just finished registering at Strayer College in Arlington. The children had adjusted well to their new schools, were doing well in their studies, and were sorry to leave. But at the end of January 1997, we moved to Baldwin, a small town in the delta of the Mississippi, close to the Gulf of Mexico. Baldwin is west of New Orleans, and about sixty miles southeast of Lafayette. UMCOR has a depot there for receiving and sending out relief supplies to the U.S. and around the world. The managers of the depot were Rex and Sherri Wyland, who arranged for our transfer. Sarah Schoeffer, a committed member of First UMC in Lafayette, was running the Sager-Brown Center. A few years later the depot and the center were merged as one entity.

The Sager-Brown Center served as a community center and a place for volunteers to receive assignments. Hundreds of retirees, young people, young adults, and college students came in response to the mission of the church, offering their gifts and graces. They spent hours sorting and packing relief items for shipment to places around the world. They also renovated homes and built new ones in the community and its environs, mainly for the elderly and the economically disadvantaged. Part of my assignment was to oversee the various aspects of the community ministry. The center offered classes in parenting, computer skills, and home maintenance, and provided food for seniors and mothers, and summer camps for children. In my time at Baldwin, the center received and shipped not only food and clothing, but also household items, school kits, and sneakers to North Korea, Liberia, Sierra Leone, Zaire, Angola, Mozambique, and Senegal.

We had a good relationship with the mayor of Baldwin, Wayne Breaux. A member of his team, Lannie Simoneaux, was a consultant to the center. The center's staff were a marvelous, dedicated bunch, whose names I have listed in appendix 8, and working together was fun and enjoyable. Irene, the children, and I had contact with thousands of Christ-centered volunteers with whom we were able to share vital information about Liberia. We even encouraged many of them to consider short-term mission opportunities in Liberia.

During 1997, I became an affiliate member of the Louisiana Annual Conference, as a clergyperson from the Liberia Annual Conference. As a result I was able to attend and participate in the 1997 and 1998 Annual Conference meetings. It was a great encouragement to know that the entire Louisiana Annual Conference was wholeheartedly committed to the work of the center. At the urging of Bishop Dan Solomon, all districts contributed relief supplies. I also became involved in activities of the Arcadian District of the conference, through District Superintendent Terry Willis. I spoke in many churches in the area around Baldwin: Lafayette, New Iberia, Jeanerette, Cherenton, Franklin, Thibodeaux, and Baldwin.

In October 1997, the Reverend Robert Osgood was named the center's director. Bob and his wife Nancy had served as UM missionaries in Haiti before coming to Sager-Brown. At that time I became chaplain for the center. Bob and I maintained an excellent working relationship and he and his wife became Irene's and my close friends. And I continued to speak about the center and about Liberia in Louisiana churches.

One church in particular, First UMC in New Iberia, pastored by the Reverend Mike McLaurin, gave valuable help to the church in Liberia. They provided scholarships for students from Grand Bassa County who were studying at the Gbarnga School of Theology. They gave $500 to purchase rice for needy Liberian UMC pastors. And they also purchased a boat engine for the Grand Bassa District to carry out pastoral work into Edina, a coastal town just a few miles north of Buchanan, via the Upper Buchanan–Edina Crossing.

The Upper Buchanan–Edina Crossing, known as the UB-EC, is the combined estuaries of the Benson, St. John, and Mechlin Rivers in Grand Bassa County. Together they form one very broad estuary that empties into the Atlantic Ocean near the historic African American settler communities of Upper Buchanan and Edina. The Reverend James D. Karblee, district superintendent of the Grand Bassa District, spent a week with us at the Sager-Brown Center during my time there, and asked us to find a church to help with UB-EC project. Thanks to the Reverend McLaurin, First Church in New Iberia responded.

Many people and churches helped our family in personal ways during our time in Baldwin. Our friend Dorethea Brown, who had brought us food during our time as evacuees in Sierra Leone, left that country when fighting broke out there in 1997, and returned to her home town, Franklin, Louisiana, just two miles from Baldwin. She made us feel very welcome. The Reverend Idella Stevenson, a pastor in the Louisiana Conference, gave us the wonderful gift of caring for our children when Irene and I needed to have some time for ourselves. How much we appreciated her love and friendship.

From my earliest days, education has been essential for me—and it has also been essential for our family. We made sure our children attended school wherever we were. First Church in New Iberia periodically donated money to help with our family's educational expenses, as did many other friends and churches both in Louisiana and in other parts of the country. I have listed these in appendix 8. Chenda graduated with honors from Franklin High School in 1998, and went on to study computer science at Central Methodist College in Fayette, Missouri, where she received a partial scholarship. The General Board of Global Ministries also gave her a leadership grant.

Janjay finished elementary school in Baldwin and went to Franklin Junior High, where she was an honor student. Blason and Bleejay both won a Drug-Free Essay Contest at Baldwin Elementary School and won brand new bicycles! Irene entered the University of Southwestern Louisiana in Lafayette as a junior, and drove our Ford Aerostar a total of ninety miles every day to and from school. She received a one-time grant of $5,000 from the UMC Women's Division based in New York.

When Trocon joined us in Baldwin from Liberia in 1997, we arranged, with the help of President Benjamin Lentz, a scholarship opportunity for him at the University of Indianapolis, where he planned to study biology. When Youjay came from Liberia in 1998, we appealed to President

James Venson of the University of Evansville, who granted him a tuition scholarship with the recommendation of Bishop Leroy Hodapp of Evansville, Indiana. Youjay's interest was international relations. Dr. William LeSeur and his wife Alene, who have since both passed away, made themselves personally responsible for Trocon and Youjay's room and board at the universities. Our other boys, Garmonyu and Genca, also graduated from high school, and later returned to Liberia where Garmonyu, at the time of this writing, was studying management at the newly established United Methodist University in Monrovia.

Many churches and individuals, more than can possibly be named in this book, deserve our profound thanks for their support and for helping with our family's education. May they find the words of St. Paul true for them: "And my God will meet all your needs according to his glorious riches in Christ Jesus" (Philippians 4:19 NIV). The Lord's goodness to us is indescribable. God's love and care go on forever.

During the years we were in Baldwin, I traveled extensively, speaking to churches in at least eleven annual conferences. (I have listed them in appendix 8.) I challenged churches and members to continue their giving to UMCOR's relief efforts around the world, and thanked them for their generous giving over the years and their advocacy for peace, justice, and human welfare in Africa and around the world. Other travel involved attending UMCOR staff meetings in New York and Arlington as well as executive training sessions in New York.

On some of these trips, Irene and the children joined me as we drove to the various assignments, and Irene helped with the driving. One of those times was our trip in June 1998 to take part in the Detroit Annual Conference held at Adrian College in Adrian, Michigan. The children were out of school and it gave us a chance for all of us to drive through a number of states and cities. On the way we stopped briefly at the University of Indianapolis to visit with Trocon.

At the conference we were part of the signing ceremony of the Covenant Document, when the covenant relationship between the Detroit Annual Conference and the Liberia Annual Conference was put in place. Irene and I, and the children, Chenda, Bleejay, Blason, and Janjay, all signed the document. Bishop Otto and Bishop Kulah also participated in the historic event. Later we were guests of the Reverend Emmanuel Giddens in St. Clair Shores, north of Detroit, at his Good Shepherd UMC parsonage.

On the way back we stopped for the night in Indianapolis, and left the next morning very early—about 4:00 A.M., driving down I-65. About thirty miles the other side of Louisville, after two and a half or three hours' drive, I stopped at a rest area. Everyone, including Irene, was asleep when I got out of the car to use the bathroom. They were still asleep—I thought—when I got back into the car and I drove back onto the highway. I didn't know that Blason and Janjay had gotten out of the car after me.

Fifty miles down the road Chenda woke up, looked at the backseat and exclaimed, "Where are the children?"

"What do you mean?" I asked.

In a trembling voice she answered, "Dad, Blason and Janjay are not in the car!"

Irene and I looked back. There were no children. Irene burst out crying. "John where are the children? What shall we do?" Bleejay and Chenda joined in the weeping.

"By God's help we'll find them," I reassured them, outwardly calm and confident, but inwardly disturbed and fearful. "Don't cry."

Irene got on the cell phone and called 911, but the police couldn't pick up the call very well. Almost immediately we were able to find a way to turn around on I-65, and at a nearby rest stop we told a worker there our story. He immediately called the police. The response was, "The children are in our care. Tell the parents not to worry, and to take their time driving because the children are in good hands."

"Praise God!" we exclaimed, laughing and crying. "God is good to us. Thank you so much," we told the gentleman who had helped us. He gave us directions on getting to the police station. What joy and happiness when we were reunited! The children told us that when they realized the car was gone, they were quite scared. A man at the rest stop told them to wait awhile, in case the car came back, and he waited with them. After some time, since we hadn't returned, he called the police for them. How grateful we were for everyone's help and for the kindness of the police. After we told friends in Baldwin about the experience, they jokingly warned us whenever we set out on a trip, "Be sure to count your family members at every rest stop!"

Another highlight was the 1998 visit of Bishop Humper from Sierra Leone to Baldwin to visit the Sager-Brown Center. After he preached at First UMC in New Iberia, that church again responded generously. The Reverend Mike McLaurin called me several days after the bishop's visit to tell me, "Our church is giving two thousand dollars toward the Bishop's Appeal for the Children of Africa."

Other travels involved visiting friends we had known earlier. In April 1998, I went to Little Rock, Arkansas, at the invitation of Bishop Bennie D. Warner, to preach in his church. Warner and his wife Anna had left Liberia in 1980 shortly before the military coup that toppled the government in which Warner was serving as vice president. When I was studying at Saint Paul's School of Theology, I had met the Warners in Syracuse, New York, where the Reverend Warner was then serving as a pastor. In the church in Little Rock I met a former Saint Paul's classmate, William Thompson, now an ordained pastor.

On another visit to Michigan I not only got to visit with my nephew, Artemus Gaye, son of my sister Esther, who was doing graduate work at Garrett Evangelical Theological Seminary in Evanston, Illinois, but I was able to attend a meeting of the Christian Extension Ministries (CEM) with which I had served back in Grand Bassa County. Henry Gueh, who had also been on the staff, and his wife Willette were now living in Kalamazoo. At our meeting were not only myself and Henry Gueh, but also the Reverend Abba G. Karnga, the Reverend Mark Scheffers, the Reverend Don Slager, Mr. Ron Gillings, and Mrs. Tim Slager. We met to plan the reopening of CEM activities in Buchanan.

In November 1998, we spent Thanksgiving with Mrs. Martha Zieler Glay in Houston. Martha had been one of the nurses who treated me when the rebels beat me up in 1993 at Camphor Mission. And right after Christmas the family joined with our friends the Tinklenbergs at his parents' place in Florida. Perry Tinklenberg had also been with Christian Extension Ministries in Monrovia. On both visits we talked over old times and praised God for the protection and goodness we had received.

On New Year's Day, 1999, I started a new appointment as UMCOR's field representative for West Africa responsible for emergency response. My primary focus was to assess the emergency needs of West Africa and report to UMCOR headquarters in the U.S. for appropriate and rapid response. I set up the office in Monrovia and installed a staff of three: Judith Dean-Walker as office assistant, Zehyu B. Wuduorgar as research assistant, and Archie Kiawu as chauffeur. They made a very good team, and we worked well together. While I started my duties immediately, the family stayed in Baldwin until the end of the school year.

Since the job was primarily a roving one, and Irene and the children had not yet completed their studies, we decided to keep our home base in the United States. We moved to Worcester, Massachusetts, because Irene's brother James was living there, and he was able to help Irene supervise the children in my absence. I made a trip to Worcester before our move and found a house there that we were able to buy.

Before we left Baldwin, the Sager-Brown family hosted a lavish send-off party in our honor, with Mayor Wayne Breaux in attendance. He presented us with a key to the town of Baldwin and named us Honorary Citizens. The center staff presented the children with a keyboard in appreciation of their musical talents displayed at the center. There was also a farewell party for us at First UMC in New Iberia. We had real sorrow at leaving Baldwin because of the bonds of affection, oneness, and spiritual growth we had experienced together.

We left Baldwin on May 24 and drove the nearly two thousand miles to Worcester, arriving two days later. Irene and I shared the driving. This time, we didn't leave any of the children at any rest stop!

James welcomed us joyfully to his home where we met his children Mada and James, Jr. We stayed with him for a week until the van arrived with our belongings. We moved into our new home on June 3. Almost immediately the Reverend Stan Culy, pastor of the Quinsigamond UMC in Worcester, visited us. The result was that we visited the church the following Sunday and eventually became active affiliate members. Janjay sang in the choir, Irene taught the classes for grades five and six, and the children joined the Sunday school. The children were given scholarships to attend Camp Aldersgate in Rhode Island. I have been privileged to participate in the worship service, and have presented the work of UMCOR to the congregation. When Stan Culy retired, the Reverend Richard Whitefleet-Smith was appointed as pastor. He and his wife JoAnn, with their two beautiful daughters, have become our good friends.

As before, we made contact with friends from Liberian days. Dr. John Kallon, former professor at the Gbarnga School of Theology, was living in the Boston area. On one of our visits to the Kallons, I served as guest preacher at the Greenwood UMC in Dorchester where they are members. We also kept in contact with former Gbarnga professors, Dr. Jefferson Labala and Dr. Daniel Brewer, who are both in the States. Whenever we called them they reminded me, "John, we are praying for you on a daily basis."

The Reverend Gwen M. Purushotham, superintendent of the Central Massachusetts District of the New England Conference, invited me to preach in a number of district churches, which I was happy to do. As a result, some of the churches were connected to the Nana Kru District of the UMC in Liberia where the Reverend Jonah Sneh was superintendent, and were able to send money and supplies to Liberia.

God was exceedingly good to us during our tour of duty both in the United States and in Africa. Through God, our ministry in America and our service with the General Board of Global Ministries was blessed. I was also able to represent the Liberia Annual Conference faithfully and conscientiously, in order to justify the trust and confidence placed in me to serve at such a high level in the Lord's vineyard. I have remained faithfully committed to the work of church, because the church has been good to us through the love of God in Jesus. I owe my Savior Jesus Christ, and my God, as well as the past and present leaders of our church, an immense debt of gratitude. I have regarded myself as under divine and moral obligation to do the work God has called me to in faith, hope, and humility.

Our family has also been very important to Irene and me. We have taken time to consider and care for the spiritual and educational needs of our children and ourselves. By our own example, we have led them in the love of Jesus Christ. They attended church regularly with us and have taken active parts in Sunday school classes in the churches we have been associated with. Many people complimented us on their good behavior, and their positive comments made Irene and me proud parents. Our children are eager to be spiritually and academically prepared for future service to their church and their country.

In concluding this chapter, I would like to say a few words about the United States, where we have lived for more than five years now. The United States is a good country, a country committed to freedom, peace, and justice for all. It is a country that opens the door of opportunities to everyone, especially the opportunity to learn. It is a country where everyone is equal before the law. No one is above the law.

The United States has concerns for world peace and justice. Oppressed people and those victimized by wars and political instability are welcomed and cared for when they ask for and receive asylum. Children are loved, respected, and protected. They learn in the best educational environments. Their rights are protected. I wish this were the case with the children of Africa. Instead, the children of Africa are abused, exploited, and manipulated by narrow-minded individuals for power and wealth. To achieve these selfish goals, they negatively indoctrinate children by drugging them and transforming them into child soldiers. These children later inflict untold atrocities and suffering on their own people. What a shame for Africa!

It is true, though, that all is not well with America. Like other countries of the world, the United States has problems. All can be well if every American will take serious and honest responsibility for the freedom God has given them. But there are many who abuse freedom through violent acts—acts that are too often portrayed on television and cinema screens. Freedom without responsibility is a hindrance to peace and justice, and can undermine the integrity of a nation. I urge every American, and every non-American who lives and works in the United States, to protect America's freedom.

God must be the source of America's freedom. God must not be left out of America's plans for global justice, peace, human rights, and freedom. Some may say that we do not need God. But the truth of the matter is that God is the creator of the universe. It is God who created America and Americans, and blessed the land and its people. Any nation that refuses to acknowledge God and does not do what God requires of it, that nation is bound to face insurmountable problems. History is the best witness.

My family and I love the United States of America. We want the United States to continue to work for world peace and justice—only depending on God as the source of her strength. We cannot do without God. God, through the church, is the source of our strength. Indeed, God's church in America has always been and will always remain the undisputed foundation of the American nation, whether Americans themselves believe it or not. No one can easily convince me that the Founding Fathers fled religious persecution in England to establish a nation that would not acknowledge the existence, omnipotence, and goodness of a loving Creator God. Certainly, America's success story did not happen by chance. It is God's answer to the prayers, the hopes, and the aspirations of those who wanted to serve God in peace and to proclaim God's love and plan of salvation for the whole human family.

One result of the American success story is the establishment of God's church in Liberia, not only by the United Methodists but also by many Christian churches from the United States. The seed has also been sown throughout Africa and many lives have been touched and transformed. America has a moral obligation to curb or minimize the vices that threaten the divine foundation of her nationhood and call into question her role as the harmonizer of global peace and stability.

World powers have flourished and then faded away because they failed to give God the glory for their greatness. May that not be true of America. America needs the fervent prayers of all true and committed Christians so that God's Word will be preached in the uttermost parts of the world.

Chapter Seventeen

My Journey to the Episcopacy

When I was elected bishop of the Liberia Annual Conference at the fifth Quadrennial Session of the West Africa Central Conference of The United Methodist Church on December 16, 2000, in Monrovia, there was great rejoicing.

But before I recount the details of the election and the events immediately preceding it, I want to look back over my life to see how the journey to the episcopacy actually started. Of course, the question of who started and completed the journey will always remain unchanged—it was God and God alone. God is the one who led me on this journey for a greater service in the ministry of Jesus Christ.

As you recall, my birth in Whayongar Town was greeted with the prediction that I would become educated and would liberate the people from the forced labor they were subjected to by the Liberian government. I did not understand the prediction and really paid no attention to it, even when the other children in the village always chose me as their leader. That was just normal playtime.

My grandparents kept predicting a bright future for me. Grandmother Kamah would often sit me on her lap to give me a traditional blessing. The blessing rite, *kordu-npopo* (or *korzu-npopu* or *kordunu-npopo,* depending on Bassa language variations) consisted of gently stroking or patting her right knee *(kordu),* while she pronounced God's blessings upon me (*npopo* means putting or placing into).

The literal interpretation of *kordu-npopo* is "putting or placing into the knee," but the symbolic meaning is the pronouncement of either a blessing or a curse. A right-knee stroke symbolizes a blessing, while a left-knee stroke symbolizes a curse. The bestowal of blessing may result from a simple act of kindness, such as giving a cup of water to someone, especially an older person who's thirsty. Weightier deeds of kindness, mercy and love induce more magnanimous right-knee stroking. Sometimes a blessing may be given because positive traits are observed in a child that could lead to future greatness or success. Thus the bestowal serves as a driving force. At other times, the blessing is given based on affection for the child. A blessing may also be given because of an unpleasant circumstance under which a child was conceived, born, or brought up. A posthumous birth, the death of the parents, a natural disaster, or war are causes for giving a blessing.

On the other hand, a curse may be pronounced for the slightest act of rudeness, disobedience, and also for the gravest show of inhumanity or wickedness. A curse may be given, for instance, because an old person or someone in distress or with a deformity has been mocked. A curse may also come from an innocent person who is being brutally killed or tortured.

Kordu-npopo may be singular or collective. The Whayongar Town blessing on me was a collective act. It implied and invoked a future in which I would become educated at all costs and eventually obtain an important position in the Liberian Government. This would earn me the needed influence and authority to shield the villagers from the ravages of others. The villagers would be my constituents or clients. Such was a common practice among Liberian settler elites and their indigenous counterparts. But the practice contained painful contradictions. Had the Whayongar Town pronouncement been fulfilled as predicted, the people in that village together with the nearby communities would have been required to render "voluntary services" to me. Such labor-intensive services would have been given for little or no wages.

My grandparents were not definite in their predictions. But they expected that I would become "someone." As time went by, I thought about their words and predictions more and more. I could see that in some way I had fulfilled these expectations. I had obtained a high level of education. I had achieved a high position by becoming a teacher and then principal of Camphor Mission after high school and college. Becoming a well-qualified educator was always my main goal. Later, I was appointed director of the mission. In the church I had become first a deacon and then a pastor. But I did not believe that the words had been real predictions of my future.

For one thing, I had a Christian upbringing from the time I was very young. I grew up in the church and in the knowledge of God and of Christian doctrine. Second, I left the traditional rural setting when I was quite young. Third, the prediction of the people of Whayongar Town was still unfulfilled. Instead of becoming a liberating politician, I was now a Christian worker. I looked at my life, my education, and my achievements as resulting from the goodness of God, not produced by *kordu-npopo.*

But later in my life, more predictions came my way—not from unlettered, rural dwellers, but from prominent and educated United Methodists, both American and African. They were predicting that I would be a bishop in The United Methodist Church. I have already mentioned the first one that came from Gretta Moffat when she visited Camphor in 1982. Ten years later, at the 159th session of the LAC held in Rivercess County, Bishop Bruce Blake of the Dallas Conference was a guest. At one point he said to me, "John, my friend, Kulah is about to retire. Who do you think will replace him?"

"There are many trained and qualified people in the LAC," I replied. "Any of them could replace him."

His response was emphatic. "*You* are going to be the one."

Also at the Rivercess Conference, Dr. Emmanuel Bailey made the same observation and repeated it later that year when I visited him at his home in Flint, Michigan, after attending the UMC General Conference.

In the three to four years following, others echoed this prediction. Not just friends like the Reverend Dr. Nathan Junius and the Reverend James D. Karblee, but coworkers like the Reverend Levi Williams, the Reverend Isaac M. Davis, and J. Larmark Cox in Monrovia, and church leaders like Bishop Robert C. Morgan of the Louisville Conference and even Bishop Kulah himself.

While I was living and working in the United States, many Liberian Methodists also caught the vision and repeatedly encouraged me to take part in the election for the LAC's episcopal leadership. (I list their names in appendix 9.) I was quite reluctant when so many brothers and sisters made these appeals, and I never actively sought the episcopacy. "What God wants to happen will happen," was my constant response. This remained the assuring theme that guided my focus even after I finally joined the other contestants in the two most decisive and unforgettable hurdles of the election process.

When Bishop Kulah officially announced his retirement at the LAC 164th session held in Gompa City, Nimba County, in 1997, Liberian United Methodists began to brainstorm on the bishop's possible replacement. In 1998, while I was still in the States, I was surprised one morning to receive from Liberia a faxed copy of the *Episcopal Drum,* with a front-page headline, "Three Persons in the Race: Reverend J. Sarwolo Nelson, Reverend Dr. Emmanuel Bailey and Reverend Dr. John G. Innis." After that people began calling me, trying to talk me into going back to Liberia in order to lay the groundwork for a successful campaign. "What God wants to happen will happen," I kept repeating. But finally, after persistent appeals, I agreed to let my name be placed on the list of candidates.

Instead of blessing and approval, however, my candidacy sparked bitter opposition, even from some of the very individuals who had predicted that I would become bishop. But that had been several years back, and times and people had obviously changed, so I wasn't too surprised when a number of those who had "blessed" me decided to contest my candidacy. What did astonish me, though, was the wave of insults and character assassinations that were thrown at me from my own United Methodist brothers and sisters.

A glimpse of this secular style of campaign strategy caught my attention when I flew back to Liberia from the U.S. to attend the 166th session of our Conference in 1999, held in Greenville, Sinoe County. I attended not only as a member of the LAC, but also as Executive Secretary of the General Board of Global Ministries. In that capacity I presented the Conference with a gift of U.S. $2,000 to help with the needs of retired pastors and widows. Quite strangely, I was never accorded the courtesy of recognition, even as an active member of our Conference. And many of my Conference brothers and sisters avoided me altogether. I was later told that they were afraid of being asked to campaign for me—something I did not do.

Two days into the Conference, I hurriedly left for Monrovia. I needed to regularize my passport because I was due shortly in Zimbabwe, to attend a training program in disaster management at Africa University. The news that reached me when I returned to the States from Zimbabwe was that I had run away from the Conference because I couldn't stand the heat that was building up with all the vicious rumors about me.

The road to the episcopacy of the Liberia Annual Conference, I realized, had a lot of hurdles to negotiate. They were man-made, I saw, and there would be more along the way to the finish line. Because they were man-made, however, and influenced by the devil, I was confident that God would clear them out of the way. So I did not give up the journey. And I did not lose courage. My faith remained firmly anchored in Jesus Christ through constant prayer and deep meditation.

God also moved the hearts of many faithful United Methodists at home and abroad to pray and fast for me. Some of them had not met me, yet they organized prayer sessions in my behalf. These prayer partners spent several sleepless nights praying with me. Many a time I heard them also praying for my adversaries. "Lord, bless those who want to destroy John Innis. Bless them abundantly so that they will forget to harm him." Some of my Lebanese and Indian friends also told me that they had me in their prayers. What a wonderful revelation! Christians and non-Christians repeatedly assured me of victory.

The 167th session of the Liberia Annual Conference of the United Methodist Church convened in February 2000 in the central highland city of Gbarnga, the provincial headquarters of Bong County. Our meetings were held in the St. John UMC, and our theme was "Forgetting the Past, Planning the Future with Hope." There was a spirit of excitement about the conference because of an item high on the agenda—the nomination of a successor to the Reverend Dr. Arthur F. Kulah, who was retiring. Dr. Kulah had served the Conference as resident bishop for twenty years—most of them with civil war in the country.

There were twelve ordained elders on the list of nominees, and each of the 959 accredited delegates had come to vote for a particular candidate. In addition, a number of United Methodist observers and other guests had come to witness this critical aspect of the Gbarnga Conference. Each of them was for individual nominees. This anticipation and concern over the voting turned the Conference into an anxiety-driven occasion where feelings ran high, particularly during the three-round voting process. As candidates were dropped for failing to obtain the required votes, their enthusiasm and that of their supporters obviously dropped. But those who made it to the next round were livelier and more confident. The rise and fall of the emotional tempo seemed an echo of the hills-and-valleys scenery of Gbarnga City.

At the end of the final round of voting, only two candidates were left to be voted on at the main election that was scheduled to take place at the 5th Quadrennial Session of the West Africa Central Conference (WACC) of the UMC. That would be in December that same year, at First United Methodist Church in downtown Monrovia. The election would be followed by the consecration of the new bishop. The candidates to be voted on were the Reverend Julius Sarwolo Nelson, Jr., and myself.

December seemed a long time away from the Gbarnga Conference for everyone concerned. But the time finally arrived. Irene flew in from the United States the day before the election, to join me for this historic time. Together on December 16, we joined an eager crowd at First UMC, an historic, two-hundred-year-old brick-and-granite structure on the corner of Ashmun and Gurley Streets in downtown Monrovia. Many people had been there for hours waiting for the voting to begin.

At 3:00 P.M. the meeting started. Our theme was "Go and Tell," and the text was Matthew 28. This time there were only sixty accredited delegates, twenty from each of the three Conferences that make up the WACC. These were the Liberia Annual Conference (LAC), the Sierra Leone Annual Conference (SAC), and the Nigeria Annual Conference (NAC).

At last the ballots were cast. Then, in the full view of the press and the Conference observers, they were carefully counted and tallied by the officiating bishops, including the presiding bishop, Dr. John Hopkins, who was the representative of the Council of Bishops of The United Methodist Church. All of us in the church were feverish with anticipation, as was the crowd waiting outside. Everyone seemed overcome by a temporary loss of self-confidence, demonstrating the truth of a popular Liberian proverb: "You are never sure of winning the game until the last whistle," or perhaps better translated, "The last whistle will determine the winner!"

With his tally pad before him, Bishop Hopkins finally broke the silence. He announced the total votes cast, and the method of tallying. "The computation of votes clearly shows that one candidate has won the election on the first ballot," he said, "the Reverend Dr. John G. Innis!"

There was a sudden deafening uproar in the church as the delegates rushed to embrace me and offer handshakes, crying "Congratulations!" and "Thank God!" One of the first to hug me was Irene, my loving and committed companion.

When the crowd outside heard the noise inside, they rushed to the windows and doors in order to find out the results. Then they too burst into a frenzy of praising and glorifying God. People were leaping for joy, singing, dancing, waving handkerchiefs in the air, shaking hands, and embracing each other. Those who could, crowded to the door of the church to try to shake my hand. Traffic was temporarily halted in that segment of Ashmun Street! God had brought to pass what I believe God had ordained for my life.

The day after the election, December 17, 2000, was a sunny Sunday afternoon. The atmosphere inside First United Methodist Church in Monrovia was calm and cordial and filled with color. United Methodists, observers and well-wishers had come en masse to witness the consecration of the bishop-elect. You could tell from the expressions on the faces of those who took part that the antagonizing spirit that had characterized the selection and election processes had melted into a singular sobriety before God.

The consecration also attracted a record-breaking crowd. A television set was placed in the conference room of the adjoining multipurpose building where the overflow crowd could watch the program live. Still a goodly number of people remained outside because of lack of space. Bishop John Hopkins, the guest preacher, delivered a soul-stirring message. Then came the consecration. Irene and I were called to the front, to kneel before the officiating bishops.

After they laid their hands on my head, I was robed and given a beautiful, tall wooden staff as the symbol of my function as a shepherd. I was then presented to the congregation as the "fourth indigenous bishop of the Liberia Annual Conference of The United Methodist Church." Clapping and shouts of "Amen!" filled the church. Irene and I embraced and kissed, registering our gratefulness to God and reaffirming our love and unhindered commitment to the ministry of our Lord Jesus Christ.

The program ended with the celebration of the Holy Eucharist. Then I was escorted again to the church's entrance, this time in the official dress of a bishop, with the staff solemnly and firmly held before me. Once again the crowd greeted me with cheers and jubilation. At last the initially meaningless predictions that had greeted my birth and come to me in childhood had become a startling reality. What a marvelous testimony to the goodness of God!

The election and consecration were climaxed by an elaborate turning-over ceremony on Wednesday, January 3, 2001. It was held at the Stephen Trowen Nagbe United Methodist Church (S.T.). This church is named after the first indigenous bishop of the UMC in Liberia. A beautiful oval structure, the S.T. stands invitingly on Tubman Boulevard between Thirteenth and Fourteenth Streets in the Sinkor, a district in southeast Monrovia. Bishop Arthur F. Kulah, the outgoing bishop, gave his farewell discourse, the church choir gave us soul-lifting songs, and more symbolic, pastoral gifts were presented to me.

My acceptance speech centered around the need to revitalize the work of The United Methodist Church in Liberia, building on the legacy of the past. The process, I suggested, would require redefined goals, perceptions, and attitudes in the spirit of love, mutual respect, and care for one another, with honesty and sincere commitment to God's work. I proposed a seven-count vision for the Liberia Annual Conference:

- A Christ-centered and spirit-filled church
- A church characterized by love for all, united in faith and service
- An evangelistically functional church
- A church whose laity and clergy are empowered to fulfill the mission of Christ
- A holistically functional church
- A church that is accountable and credible
- A church characterized by integrity, honesty, and faithfulness

I used to say that the declarations of the people in Whayongar Town, including my grandparents, had no relevance to the positive unfolding events of my life. But I became convinced at last that it was God who spoke through my grands and the people of Whayongar Town. Though I did not become the kind of liberator the town folks predicted, the education I acquired and the positions I occupied fulfilled their predictions in other ways. Hundreds of young people, particularly those from rural areas, were freed from the bondage of illiteracy and backwardness so prevalent among our people. Many rural dwellers, as well, heard and accepted the message of freedom from sin and the gift of eternal life through Jesus Christ.

The collective knee-patting of the people of my maternal village finally taught me a significant lesson. A vision may not necessarily be fulfilled as expected, but as implied. Perhaps my episcopal journey did begin the very day I was born in Whayongar Town.

Chapter Eighteen

Brothers and Sisters

Throughout this book I have tried to remember many of the people who have influenced my life, from the remote village of Whayongar Town in Grand Bassa County, Liberia, to the advanced countries of America, Europe, and other parts of the world. This chapter, however, is reserved for my immediate family members. I have added it for three main reasons.

First, it is an acknowledgment of a unique aspect of the cultural environment in which I was born and bred: that is, the strong emphasis placed on blood relation which begins with the immediate family and stretches to an almost endless genealogy of distant relations. Second, I want readers to know the children born to my father. Third, I want to pay homage to all of us for our complementary roles as brothers and sisters striving to ensure love, unity, and betterment for each of us.

As I mentioned in chapter 1, our father, Philip Dwah Innis, had fourteen children, five girls and nine boys. The girls are: Juah, Sundaymah, Esther, Yeadoe (Sayyea), and Felicia. The boys are: James, Nathaniel, Roosevelt, Dwahyuway, Jerry, William, Patrick, Teedoe, and myself.

Juah, who died in 1995 from a brief illness, was the oldest of the children. I still cherish sweet memories of her; she was a kind, loving, and caring sister who assisted me as she was able from her meager means. Juah was married twice. Her first husband, David Wonto, was very fond of me, and assisted me with food and clothing when I was in elementary and junior high school. Juah and David had a girl named Sayneh. They later divorced and she married Bonwein Logan. They have two children, Paul and Mardea.

Juah encouraged me to acquire an education that would benefit the family and continued to help me until I completed college.

Sundaymah and her husband John Soclo also provided support for me from elementary school through college. They were blessed with seven children: Amelia, John Soclo, Jr., Lydia, Samuel, Kpah, Emmanuel, and Torrkpa.

Much has already been said about the vital role my brother James played in my education, starting with his tutoring me when I returned from Monrovia without any knowledge of the alphabet or numerals. My gratitude for James would be incomplete, however, if I didn't mention his family. He has been married for more than twenty years to plump and charming Vivian Musu Scott, and the marriage is crowned with six promising children: James Innis, Jr., Williametta, Philip II, Nijay, Amy, and Tomah. *Tomah* is a *Bahsor* word that means "war woman" or "woman of war," and she was born during the Liberian Civil War. James Innis, Jr., graduated from the University of Liberia with a B.B.A. in Management, and was a freshman student at the University's Louis Arthur Grimes School of Law when this book was being written.

The rest of my brothers and sisters were not in a position to help me as were my older siblings. Some were themselves in school, while a number were still under age. Instead we, the older ones, provided educational and other assistance since we were able to. Yet the fact that they didn't make a financial contribution towards our education doesn't mean that they were insensitive to the effort we were making. They regarded us as the pride of the family, and their moral support helped us muster more courage and determination to keep forging ahead. Some of my brothers and sisters lived with me, particularly when I became principal and director of Camphor Mission, as well as during my tenure as administrative assistant to Bishop Kulah.

Over the years, James and I had the pleasing duty of playing the fatherly role and encouraging our brothers and sister to become educated. The positive outcome of our effort has given us much joy and satisfaction. Esther, for instance, has a high school diploma and a certificate in home economics from the Asian Rural Institute in Japan. She is also a longtime family woman. She is married to Borbor Gaye, a former famous Liberian soccer star who is deputy minister at the Ministry of Youth and Sports. They have two children, a daughter, Zoe, who is hoping to enroll at the University of Liberia, and a son, Artemus, who is in the U.S. working on a master's degree.

Nathaniel holds a B.Sc. in economics from University of Liberia. He became a teacher at Camphor Mission and acted as the school's principal during my study leave in America. He was later appointed assistant superintendent for development of Grand Bassa County. At the time of writing this book, he was director for domestic trade at the Ministry of Commerce and Industry in Monrovia. Nathaniel is married to beautiful Yvonne Diggs and they have two children, Trokonjay and Nathaniel, Jr.

Felicia is the proud holder of a B.Sc. in biology, a course of study generally dreaded by the average Liberian student, and was planning to enroll in medical school as this book was being written. William has an associate degree in accounting from the UMC Junior College of West Africa in Monrovia and was continuing at the United Methodist University created in 1998. Roosevelt and Jerry were working toward diplomas in theology and Christian education at the Gbarnga School of Theology. Patrick attended UMU, while Teedoe was a senior high school student.

It is also appropriate in this chapter to recognize a number of maternal and paternal cousins who have been important parts of my life and who have made me feel very special to them. I am especially grateful to Ruth Neor who lived with Irene and me from age seven until her graduation from high school. I am also indebted to her two older sisters, Betty and Zoe. I must mention as well my paternal cousins Cecelia, Yumonzu, Muaye-yea and Gbehzohnmeh. Then there are Borbor Mason and the Kayfoains: John, Arthur, Frances, Janjay, and James. All of these cousins of mine have been in some way regarded as brothers and sisters, and I have appreciated their concern and respect for me. For all of us, our relationship as brothers and sisters and cousins has improved our lives.

Chapter Nineteen

The Church's Influence

Imagine that you belong to a very wealthy, generous, and caring extended family. In this noble family, you were cared for from birth until you became fully adult. You were taught how to treasure the dignity of labor, how to behave well. You were enabled to acquire a good education. Not only did this remarkable family tradition provide you with a successful marriage and a well-paid job, but it also provided you with rights and privileges that could not have been otherwise possible. And so you became an asset and a pride to your family and to your community. Yet despite the kind, loving, and caring efforts of your family, you repeat to yourself, "The family has done nothing for me." What an outrageous ingratitude that would be!

I am that ingrate—or at least I was, until I realized that I had been exhibiting one of the negative attitudes the apostle Paul predicted in 2 Timothy 3—ungratefulness. So this chapter is both a confession of guilt as well as a description of the Church's positive role in making me what I am today.

Before I graduated from college, I had the erroneous notion that The United Methodist Church had done nothing for me. That was still my view when I enrolled in seminary. But one day, as I began to reflect upon my life's journey from childhood to the present, the mask of ingratitude fell from my mind's eye. For the first time it dawned on me that I had actually nurtured a wrong perception of the church. Through Jesus Christ, the church had done more for me than I could imagine.

So I began to ask myself a number of questions: "Why did I feel the way I felt about the church until now? What were the motivating factors? Was I unrealistically repeating a popular view held by most church members who expect the church to give them everything on a platter? Or was I acting out of my own free will?"

The answer that came to my mind was that of personal guilt, regardless of what had prompted me to develop such a false feeling about the church. Now, in this chapter, I want to acknowledge the goodness of God to me through the church by giving concrete examples.

As you know, I was born to United Methodist parents, both members of the Camphor Memorial MC. My maternal grandparents, Glor and Kamah, were also United Methodists, members of the St. John UMC in Neepu Clan, Grand Bassa County, where I was born and raised until I was eight. In their desire for me to grow up in the knowledge and love of God, my grands had me baptized at a very young age. Baptism is an avenue through which a person enters and is received into the faith community. So when Grandpa Glor and Grandma Kamah led me to become a part of the community of believers in God, they not only fulfilled their responsibilities as faithful disciples and loving grandparents, they also set me on a journey that would yield great dividends for me. Though I was too young to understand it at the time, I never betrayed their efforts. From the time that they presented me to the Church and the members received me, I have remained and grown in the understanding of God's purpose for my life.

An early example of the church's positive influence on my life was my childhood practice of imitating a reverend when I played at being the pastor of our mock childhood church. God, through the Church, later transformed that childhood aspiration into a reality.

When my parents divorced, I had to leave my grands and live with my father, who sent me straight to Camphor Mission to begin my education. Although my stay there was very brief, yet the morning and evening devotions helped to water my germinating spiritual growth. That growth continued to be nurtured when I returned to

Camphor from Monrovia. This time I started school in earnest and remained there until I had completed the sixth grade. During those years, my father taught me how to read the Bible both at home and in the church services. He also taught my brother James and me how to record and read our church's minutes. An added advantage was that my dad took me to many Conference and church meetings throughout Bassaland.

The dual educational and spiritual influence of Camphor Mission on my life might not have been possible without the foresight of those Christian fathers and mothers whose concern gave birth to the Mission. Bassa MC leaders led by the late Reverend George Goodside Dean established Camphor in 1947. The Reverend Dean is considered the father of Methodism among the Bassa ethnic group of Liberia. Though these church leaders themselves lacked Western educations, they were great men and women with vision. They wanted to build a mission station for the education of their children. They knew that in the future their children would become leaders in the church. Many others, like the Reverend James Karblee, and I have been the beneficiaries of their dream. With the prayers and support of the Camphor Church we completed our studies at the Mission.

With the same prayers and support of the Camphor Church, I moved to Buchanan City for high school. There I became actively involved in the activities of the Whitfield UMC. During my high school days, the Reverend James A. Griggs, a pastor in the Grand Bassa District (formerly the Group A District) spotted us potential future leaders and worked with us. On one occasion, he invited James and me to attend and participate in a weeklong evangelistic crusade in Fortsville, Grand Bassa County. We were happily accommodated in the home of Henry and Mary Adams. Through their love and kindness to us they demonstrated what it really means to be united in Christ.

Another example of the Church's influence on my life was my being employed by the LAC's Department of

Education to teach at Camphor Mission in 1971 after I graduated from high school. While serving as a teacher, I also took part in the work of Camphor Church, particularly with the young people. The outcome of my involvement in the life of the school and the church was a scholarship award from the Conference to study at the University of Liberia.

At the university, the UMC head office employed me as a cadet first in the Youth Department and later in the Department of Education. After university, the Conference again employed me, this time as principal of Camphor Mission. My tenure there provided me with many wonderful opportunities to come in contact with influential UMC leaders and members as well as with members of other churches both at home and abroad. These contacts contributed greatly to the physical and educational development of the school and the Camphor Church. In my own life, the Church began to play an even more important role when the Reverend G. Solomon Gueh licensed me in 1984 as a local pastor. Later he appointed me as pastor of Camphor Memorial UMC, now Garfield UMC.

The Church then granted me, for the second time, a scholarship to pursue graduate studies abroad. During that time I had many opportunities to meet outstanding United Methodists—bishops, president of seminaries, pastors, doctors, children, youth, young adults. My interaction with these good Christian folk had a positive impact on the overall development of Camphor Mission.

After helping me to obtain my Master of Divinity degree at Saint Paul School of Theology, the church continued to bless me. When I returned to Camphor, my job title was changed to director of Camphor Mission. In 1989, at its Annual Conference held in Greenville, Sinoe County, Bishop Arthur J. Kulah ordained me a deacon. In 1991 Bishop Kulah ordained me an elder and I was officially appointed as pastor of the Garfield UMC.

Over the years I was able to gain experience as well as serve the Church in a number of voluntary activities.

During high school (1965–1970) I served as associate district secretary for the St. John River District (UMC). During my sophomore and junior years I was secretary for the UM Youth Fellowship (LAC). Also, as a high school student, I was five times a lay delegate from Camphor Memorial UMC to the Annual Conference (LAC). In Buchanan, I was president of the youth fellowship at Whitfield Memorial UMC for four years.

While I was studying at Saint Paul School of Theology, I served the Liberia Association of Greater Kansas City as secretary and chaplain. After I returned to Liberia I continued to serve the church and the LAC in various ways. From 1989–1996, I was chairperson of the Council on Ministries for the LAC. In 1992, I was a delegate to the West Africa Central Conference in Moyamba, Sierra Leone. That same year I also attended the UMC General Conference, held in Louisville, Kentucky, as an observer. In 1993, I was a delegate to the Methodist Conference of Nigeria. From 1992–1996, I served as chair of the Committee on Episcopacy for the West African Central Conference. From 1993–1996, I was secretary of the Board of Ordained Ministries for the Liberia Annual Conference. For the years 1993–1995, I was acting district superintendent of the St. John River District, UMC, and from 1993–1996 was a member of the executive committee of the LAC. In all of these ways, the church gave me the opportunity to learn and grow.

While I was working with the General Board of Global Ministries in the United States, I obtained two additional degrees to improve my academic qualifications and skills: a Ph.D in Church Administration and a Ph.D in Christian Leadership Development. In February 1999, I received a Ph.D. in Church Administration from the Institute for Christian Works in Washington State. Then in January 2000, I received a Ph.D. in Christian Leadership from Columbus University in Nefaire, Louisiana.

During the 1980s the leaders of the Christian Education Foundation (CEF) in Grand Bassa were impressed by what was going on at Camphor. They subsequently appointed me executive director of Christian Extension Ministries (CEM)—one of the Foundation's subsidiaries. CEM is an ecumenical organization funded by the Christian Reformed Church of North America. My appointment was also based on the desire of the board to localize the CEM's leadership. My appointment would not have been possible without the earlier influence the leaders and members of the Bassa Christian community had on my life. The Reverend Abba G. Karnga of the World Wide Mission Church and the Reverend John Dorsu Kono of St. Mark's AME Church were two of the important ones.

Under my leadership, we cultivated an exuberant spiritual working relationship with both the local and expatriate CEM staff members. The local staff was comprised of the Reverend Henry G. Gueh, Mrs. Gladys Kaiser-Aye, the Reverend Seokin Payne, Peter Glay, Amos Gbah, Solomon Forkay, and Robert Glaygbo. The expatriates were Perry Tinklenberg, Mark Sheffers, Tim Slager, Joe Owns, and Don Slager.

With an annual budget of U.S. $144,000, CEM had programs in agriculture, primary health care, leadership development, literacy, and Bible translation. We also completed and fully equipped a radio station in Buchanan City that was slated to begin broadcasting on May 2, 1990. Unfortunately, because of the civil war, it never opened. It was completely looted by NPFL rebels after they captured the city in May and was made one of their military strongholds.

When the civil war finally uprooted us from Camphor into Monrovia, the church still extended her hands of benevolence to my family and me. We were hosted at the lovely Twelfth Street UMC compound and I was given the post of administrative assistant to the bishop. Here again I was brought into contact with national and international leading UMC personalities. And I developed close personal and spiritual relationships with many of the local pastors including the Reverend Dr. Nathan Junius, the Reverend Levi C. Williams, II, the Reverend Anna Kpaan, the Reverend Momoh Kpaah, the Reverend John Russell, the Reverend Julius Nelson, and the Reverend David Doe. We had a great working relationship among the staff at the head office. And I very much enjoyed my fellowship with the students at Gbarnga School of Theology where I was a lecturer.

While working for the church with the bishop, I was able to maintain contact with the UMC in Germany, as well as with other philanthropic organizations abroad. And when I joined the General Board of Global Ministries in 1996 as one of its executive secretaries, I was afforded the opportunity to travel to several countries—Mozambique, Zimbabwe, Canada, France, Côte d'Ivoire, Sierra Leone, Ghana, and Zaire—where I met many fine Christians. And of course, while I was at seminary and later working in the United States, I was privileged to visit many states on the church's business, and meet many thousands of people, both Christian and non-Christian, who had a wonderful impact on my life. All this the church has given me.

This book would be incomplete if I didn't mention the Reverend S. Trowen Nagbe, the first indigenous bishop of the Liberia Annual Conference. It was he, together with Bishop Bennie D. Warner and the Reverend Dr. Arthur F. Kulah, who identified me as a potential leader of the UMC. These three men gave me spiritual direction through their wise counsel, encouragement, and support. I owe them an immense debt of gratitude. There are several laypeople I should mention who helped me, in particular: Ambassador S. Edward Peal, Dr. Joseph Toga, Sr., Mrs. Gertrude Brewer, Miss Evelyn Cassell, Old Lady Mary Freeman, Titi Flahn-Gbayu. So many people blessed me and encouraged me through kind words in my walk with Jesus.

I need to make special mention of my wife, Irene, before concluding this chapter on the church's influence. Irene, like myself, was born to Christian parents. Our similar backgrounds, and the somewhat miraculous beginning of our relationship made us feel that God meant for us to become true life partners. I am most grateful to God for the influence of the church and for Irene's Christian commitment, consistency, and advisory role.

In the light of all that I have written throughout the book and summarized here, how would I dare say that the church did not do anything for me? On the contrary, I affirm that God, through the church, has been the source of my being and doing. But even before the church helped me, God first preserved my life through the prayers and blessings of many. When my mother left me in Whayongar Town, a nursing baby to feed on my grandmother's breasts, I could have died due to lack of needful nutrients. But I survived through God's grace. God repeatedly protected and saved my life—when I became a wayward child in Monrovia, when I returned to Bassa by rowboat on the unpredictable ocean, when I survived the beating and the fighting in the brutal Liberian Civil War.

This chapter is not intended to paint a perfect picture of a "good guy." Rather it is an attempt to give God the glory in a practical way, by showing all the good things God has done for me. God helped me to come to grips with my pride and gave me the will power to admit that I had wronged God and others. "All have sinned," says the apostle Paul, "and fall short of the glory of God" (Romans 3:23 NRSV). But, thank God, through Jesus Christ, "if we confess our sins, he is faithful and just to forgive us our sins" (1 John 1:9 KJV). The recognition of God's all-encompassing love and kindness to me is what prompted the title of this autobiography: "By the Goodness of God."

Epilogue

PRESSING ON

Looking back over my life has filled me with deep gratitude for God's loving-kindness and goodness to me through the years. Now that I have written this book and dedicated it to the honor and glory of God, what is my response? What am I to do now?

I am resolved to *keep pressing on*. That is the pledge of my loyalty and total commitment to God's ministry in Jesus Christ through the church. God has been and continues to be the source of my being. So I will continue not only to acknowledge God's goodness but will also respond to God's loving-kindness by humbly and willingly walking in loyalty to God and in service to God's people through the church.

"Whoever wishes to be great among you must be your servant. . . . I am among you as one who serves," Jesus told us (Matthew 20:26; Luke 22:26-27 NRSV). Those who are called and set apart by God to serve well to the honor and glory of God must have the Spirit of the servant Christ upon them. To be a servant of God in Jesus Christ means that whatever gift of leadership God has given us must be used to help strengthen our sisters and brothers and those who are weak and helpless. We must faithfully and generously share the goodness we have received; "freely ye have received, freely give" (Matthew 10:8 KJV). John Wesley fully understood this divine appeal when he said to the people of God that we should do good to people of all races, tribes, and nationalities—at all times and in all places.

Jesus commissioned the Twelve to make disciples of all persons, all nations (Matthew 28:19). We are not to consider their race or tribe, their social, economic, or political background. Since the church has equipped and blessed me for this same purpose, I am under oath never to discriminate, directly or otherwise, against any of God's people. As the songwriter reminds us:

We are one in the Spirit,
We are one in the Lord.

As God's children we must make a difference in others' lives by showing them our Christian love. My "pressing on" implies that I am prepared to minister to others both within and outside the church. I will create caring and uplifting relationships by detecting, affirming, harnessing, and valuing the special gifts of God's people for the ultimate realization of God's mission and purpose for our lives.

So I present this book, not as a mere life story to be read and forgotten, but as a challenge to myself and to all of us to reaffirm God's boundless love and concern for each member of the human family, regardless of who we are or where we come from. "Pressing on" is not just a lip-service vow. It is a statement of my sincere pledge to strive for perfection in my being and doing for God. "Pressing on" means that my life will be totally under the influence of God in Christ. It is therefore my desire that as I "press on," I will always serve God and God's people with love and care.

May the peace and the love of God be with all who will prayerfully read this book and meditate upon it.

Appendixes

Appendix 1
BAHSOR CHILDREN'S GAMES, SONGS, AND CHANTS

Leg-Counting Chant

Bloo bloo
Yaa yaa
Bloo bloo
Yaa yaa
Ah doh gheh doh gheh mahn yah gbo
Gafo yea deh duo duo kuehn
Kio kio bladeh bgo
Dahnmahn dahnmahn yi ni kabuaye blah
Zaykay mahntu yauhn peh peh-o-way dahn kpleh
Ah yehn mehn yehn mehn yi ni tu tu blah
titi ayi ni gbehdeh blah
Dhay tadohn vio, dhay bogborhn vior
❄ ❄ ❄ ❄ ❄

The Yellow Rice Bird Song

Booga, booga
Blay-eh ni daye daye

Konyon whoe-doe-yuah nyu whaye
Mdohn ni who-doe-yuah-nyu hehn.
❄ ❄ ❄ ❄ ❄

Brown Pigeon Chant 1

Glaygho drin jay zon-nzon?
Gbehzohn buikpo tu sehn.
❄ ❄ ❄ ❄ ❄

Brown Pigeon Chant 2

This chant is a family discussion between the male pigeon and his wife. Notice the contrast between the laziness of the male pigeon (MP) and the resentment of the female pigeon (FP). It too plays on the cooing sounds of the pigeons.

MP: Ni gbahn-way ah po sahdah aye.

FP: Ah po sada poo deh ah kaye dayeh?

MP: Ahn zor ahn daye?
Ahn zor ahn daye?

FP: Zordeh—or jaye?
Zordeh—or jaye?

MP: Zuu poaye boo.
Zuu poaye boo.

MP: Dear wife, let's build a kitchen stall for rice.

FP: A kitchen stall for rice we'll build.
What provision shall we store within?

MP: Can't we beg for what we store?
Can't we beg for what we store?

FP: For beggars' provision sake?
For beggars' provision sake?

MP: *Zip*—pour in okra sauce.
Zip—pour in okra sauce.

I've used the word *zip* to represent the Bassa word *zuu*, which represents the sound made by pouring liquid into a container.

❄ ❄ ❄ ❄ ❄

A Spider Story

Once upon a time in a village lived Spider and Little Boy. One day Spider said to Little Boy, "We're almost in the middle of the rainy season. The river and creeks will soon be overflowing their banks and running through the nearby undergrowth. That's when the fish usually leave the rivers and search the tributaries for food. So let's build a *dehgbo* across a small tributary and catch as many fish as possible."

[A *dehgbo* is a fence or weir across a stream or river to catch fish. It is constructed of mats or thatch, firmly supported by sticks and twine, with several openings at the base where raffia baskets or hollow bamboo logs are fitted to trap the fish.]

"That's a great idea, Mr. Spider," said Little Boy. And together they built the fence, though Little Boy did most of the work.

That night there was a mild shower, which pleased Spider. Early in the morning, he ran to Little Boy's home, woke him up, and they both went to the creek to check their fence. The baskets were half filled with fish.

Now Little Boy knew that Spider was greedy, mean, and cunning. So he knew from the beginning that what Spider really wanted was to use Little Boy to build the fence, and then to find a way to steal the fish. So he decided to trap Spider with his own craftiness and greed.

"Mr. Spider," Little Boy said, "you can have the first catch of fish because you are older. According to our tradition, the one who first sees daylight at birth must take the lead. Tonight, though, we should have a heavier rain, so tomorrow's catch will certainly be more."

"How dare you think you can fool a wise and mature person like me?" Spider said angrily. "Who do you think is entitled to more fish? Is it not I?"

So Little Boy gladly took the fish home to his parents. They shared some with the neighbors, cooked a portion, and preserved the rest by smoking it over the fire on a dryer.

That night there was a heavy downpour of rain. When Spider and Little Boy rushed to the fence in the morning, the baskets were full of fish. Little Boy again offered Spider the day's catch, but Spider insisted that the boy should take the fish. The huge quantity to be caught the following day would be his.

On the third morning when Spider and Little Boy reached the fence the water had receded to ankle level. All the baskets were overstuffed with fish, and more fish were swimming helplessly in the shallow water in front of the fence. These Spider and Little Boy easily killed with their machetes. They made *kinjahs,* carrying pouches, out of thatch and packed all the fish into them. There were several *kinjahs* full, and again Little Boy offered to let Spider have all the fish. Again Spider insisted that Little Boy take them. "I'll wait for the biggest catch of all tomorrow," he said. So

Little Boy, with Spider's help, carried the fish home, and there was plenty to eat and share with the people of the town.

In the evening, the sky was covered with black clouds so thick the lightning hardly shone through. Everyone predicted an enormous downpour of rain. Spider quickly went to bed, imagining his great fortune in the morning. All night it rained furiously. Spider was so delighted and excited, he couldn't sleep. He kept counting the many *kinjahs* of fish that would be his the next day.

Very early in the morning Spider hurried to wake up Little Boy. But when they got to the creek, not only the main river but also all the tributaries had overflowed their banks in a great flood. The entire *deghbo* fence had been swept away by the ferocious current.

Bitterly disappointed, Spider crossed his hands over his head and wept.

Appendix 2

Bassa High School Faculty

I am deeply grateful to all the members of the Bassa High School faculty during my years there. Mr. Richard Daker, Mr. Samuel Findley, Miss Joyce Garring (a Peace Corps volunteer), Mrs. Esthel Harris, Mrs. Lattie Harmon, Mr. Nathanial Hodge, Mr. Bloh Howard, Mr. Slomon Mah, Mrs. Doris McCritty, Mrs. Mary V. M. Reeves, Mr. Jeremiah Reeves, Prof. Beldev Singh, Mr. Knowlen Stowell (also a Peace Corps volunteer), Mrs. Helen Summerville, Mr. Alexander Vivour. All of these encouraged us to compete for academic excellence and would not allow us to slack off.

Yet despite their sternness, they were understanding in handling students' problems.

Bassa High School Classmates

Asetta Allison and David Jallah were two of my classmates who transferred to other high schools outside of Grand Bassa County.

Gallow Roberts, Augustus Reeves, Edward J. Harris, Jr., David Mason, Jacob Kaiser, and Joseph Kilby were among the key soccer players of our tenth grade class.

Others who were fellow students during my six years at Bassa High, in addition to the four who graduated with me and those mentioned above, were Thomas Bernard, Euphemia Flood, John Gibson, Annie Harris, Joseph Harris, Charles Hennings, Henry Huducker, David Jallah, Miama Jallah, Marie Lloyd, Matilda Kilby, Alfreda Morgan, Frankie Morris, Wilmot Morris, Herbert Reeves, Carolyn Smith, Harrison Somah, James Sorbor, and Stafford Torbor.

Top Quizzers at Bassa High

David Cole, Onnesmus Gayeman, Mark Karnga, Mary Karnga, Rogee Morris, Harrison Somah, Paul Tarr, Ozinga Wuduehyu, and Zehyu Wuduorgar were among the top Youth for Christ quizzers while I was at Bassa High.

Generous Church Members Who Helped Me in High School

Mr. A. B. Cleon, my granduncle Gbor Clinton and his family, Cousin Dehnsaykon, the Reverend and Mrs. Early,

Titi Flahn-Gbawheedee, Gbarwheedee Gbadyu, Mayda Gbadyu, James Harris, Joseph Harris, Siatta Harris, Robert Redd, Annie Strong, Esther Strong, Kin-yonnon Strong, John Moses K. Wheh.

Appendix 3

Friends and Family Who Helped Me in My University Years

A. B. Cleon, James Moses Deshield, David Freeman, Joe Garkpa, Mahnday Giahquee, Hawa Gibson, James Mingle, Nathan Mingle, Ruben Mingle, the Hon. Gee L. Roberts. Family members: Uncle Levi, Uncle Bobor, Gbawheedee Bgedyu, Titi Flahn, Cousin John David, my sister Juah, my sister Sundaymah and her husband John Soclo, Aunt Sorday, Aunt Julie and her husband, Richard Marshall, Conway Gartayn and Samuel Gaye.

University Professors Whom I Appreciated

Mrs. Theodora Ward-Jackson, dean; Dr. Mary Antoinette Grimes-Brown-Sherman, vice-president for academic affairs; Dr. Thomas Koon, educational methodology; Dr. Harold Kofi Lawrence, history; Dr. Amos Sawyer, political science; Professor Abraham James, political science; Mrs. Danieletta Bracewell, dean of student affairs and professor of education psychology; Dr. Frederick Gbebge, practice teaching; Professor C. Wesley Armstrong, public administration; Dr. Thomas Bestman, tests and measurement;

Professor George Flahn, mathematics and statistics; Dr. Solomon Russell, mathematics; Professor Yancy Peter Flahn, history.

Some Bassa Student Association Members at the University

Charles Gould, Theophilus Gould, James B. Logan, Charlene Reeves, Arthur Russell, Mardea Tarr, Zehyu B. Wuduorgar.

Students Who Graduated with Me from the University of Liberia

Ehuphemia Adullah, Emmanuel Bowier, Moore E. James, Maxwell Kaba, Joseph Korto, Alhaji Kromah, Cletus Nappy, Jaryenneh Moore, Mary Okai, Femo Roberts, Alfred Thomas.

Appendix 4

Camphor Mission School Ninth Grade Students 1981–1984

(based my my best recollections and the input of former students)

Class of 1981

Comfort Chenekin
Randolph Cooper
Paul Dean
Emmanuel Johnson
Joseph Kayfoain
Moses Kpoesuah
Arthur S. Neor
Emanuel Nyankan

Abraham Frank
Charles Gray
Peter G. Clay
Marcus Higgins
Julia Kulah
Rocheford Ledlo
Peter Mor
Isaac Nathan
Isaac Padmore
Jerome Page
Samuel Paygar
Lewis Vambo
Scia Varney
Nathaniel B. Zehyu

Class of 1982

Albert Barchue
Annie Crusoe
Nathaniel Hodge
Roosevelt W. Innis
Mary-Ann Johnson
Boimah Kromah
Moses Lewis
Amos Mandah
Johnson Quallah

Class of 1983

Anthony B. Cephas
Paul K. Cephas
Henry B. Cooper
Jerry W. Innis
Joseph John
Ruben D. Neor
David Reah
Joseph N. Sayuo
Alphonso B. Teah
Sebron B. Toegar, Jr.

Class of 1984

Hannah Andrews
Joseph Freeman
Elizabeth Gargar
Daniel Harmon
James G. Innis, Jr,
Esther Krayngar
Jacob Nathan
Betty Neor
James Y. Smith
Emma Summerville
Jonathan Vambo

Camphor Mission School Faculty, 1978–1984

John G. Innis, Principal
G. Solomon Gueh, Vice Principal, Bible Teacher
Alvin Thomas, Teacher, Faculty Advisor

Annie Early, Business Manager
Samuel Peterson, Registrar
Samuel B. Kaykay, Vice Principal
Augustus D.Williams, Vice Principal
John M. Barlinyu, Registrar
Edward S. Philips, Agriculture Teacher
Eric B. Gbarwheon, Teacher
Mark B. Ellis, Teacher
Isaac Chupkue Padmore, Teacher
Nathaniel B. Zehyu, Teacher
J. Shadrack Nimely, Teacher

Appendix 5

Friends Who Graced Our Wedding

Groomsmen:

Conway Gartayn, Nathaniel Weah, David Zeon, Eric Gbarwheon, Solomon Glay.

Bridesmaids:

Nyeanah Zeigler, Joanna Thomas, Sarah Page, Chadi Toll, Esther Krangar, Janice Kilby.

Other friends and helpers:

Martha Z. Glay, Ella L. Jallah, Emmalyn Junius-King. Mrs. Caroline Voger and Mrs. Peggy Charles made the wedding cake. They are the wives of two of our missionary friends at the Christian Education Foundation.

Appendix 6

1988 Graduates from Camphor Mission

James Gbordoe, Youjay Innis, Trocon Innis, Richmond Sadatonou, Nagbe Sagbe, Matthew Vambo, Joe Ghiawhee, Bob Kpleh, Veronica Gardea, Mercy Cooper.

1989 Graduates from Camphor Mission

Elmos Glay, Oretha Printer, Debora Nuka, Besy Wroh, William Mah, Nemeyu Sagbe, Jessie Smith.

Appendix 7

Gifts from the Garfield Congregation and Other Friends and Family

(when we were stranded in Buchanan during the April 1996 war)

Donors of food and other items

Aletha Barboingar
Mr. and Mrs. Joseph Beerdeh
Naomi Brooks
Mrs. Esther Innis
Sayyea Innis
Mrs. Emmalyn Junius-King

Rev. J. C. Early, Sr.	Mr. and Mrs. Matthew
Emma Ghiah	Mr. Sam Nasser
Mini Glay	Mr. and Mrs. Edward Philips

Donors of monetary gifts (Liberian dollars)

Garfield UMC	$2,000
Treasurer, St. John River District	300
Whifield UMC	500
Howard UMC	50
P. D. Innis UMC Family	100
Camphor UMC Mission/School	1,000
Buchanan First UMC	200
Christian Extension Ministries Health Center	500
Pastor Alfred W. Page, Jr.	500
Mr. and Mrs. Eric Davis	100

Appendix 8

UMCOR Staff Connected with the Sager-Brown Center in Baldwin, Louisiana

Leo Baker	Adrienne Johnson
Roger and Beverly Bard	Hazel Jones
Dick and Maribel Blair	Ginny and Ora Krieder
Gale Bolidore	Steve Most
Virginia Bonoomme	Terry and Sybil Park
James Brook	Linda and Herb Reckling
Gwen Druilhet	Wanda Scott
Betty Foulcord	Julana Senette
Fran and Richard Green	Richard and Barbara Sockrider

Tina Jack
Mary Jenkins
Rex and Sherri Wyland

Wendy Whitside was our contact in New York.

Churches and Individuals Who Contributed to Our Family's Education

Mrs. Patricia Akrabawi, Temple UMC, Evansville, Indiana
Ulrike and Martin Boehringer, Germany
Claudia and Bill Boelte, New Iberia, Louisiana
Miss Dorethea Brown, Franklin, Louisiana
Jim Coy, Beacon Group, Evansville, Indiana
Bishop and Mrs. Sheldon Ducker, Indiana
First UMC, New Iberia, Louisiana
First UMC, Ormand Beach, Florida
Garfield Memorial UMC, Pepper Pike, Ohio
Hope UMC, Belchertown, Massachusetts
Nelson Memorial UMC, Boonville, Missouri
Mrs. Jane Otto, Two Rivers, Wisconsin
Quinsigamond UMC,Worcester, Massachusetts
Jim and Nedra Starkey
St. Paul's UMC, Tucson, Arizona
Southport UMC, Indianapolis, Indiana
United Parish, Fitchburg, Massachusetts
Mr. and Mrs. Sam White, New Iberia, Louisiana

Annual Conferences in the U.S. Where I Spoke to Local Churches

Detroit, East Ohio, Eastern Pennsylvania, Iowa, Minnesota, North Carolina, Oregon-Idaho, South Carolina, South Indiana, Western Pennsylvania

Appendix 9

Liberian United Methodists Living in the United States Who Urged Me to Take Part in the Election

The Reverend John Brachard, the Reverend Roland Clarke, the Reverend Rose Cummings, the Reverend Solomon G. Gueh, the Reverend Matthew A. Jiah, the Reverend Priscilla Jiah, the Reverend Dr. Jefferson Labala, Dr. John Kallon, the Reverend Dermacus Mulbah, the Reverend John McCulley.

Voting Records of the Gbarnga Nominations at the 167th Sessions, LAC/UMC

Conference Journal of the One Hundred Sixty-Seventh Session of the Liberia Annual Conference, United Methodist Church, Gbarnga City, Bong County, Liberia, February 7-13, 2000, pp. 205-220.

Round One—Preliminary

In the preliminary round, many individuals were nominated from the floor by others who believed in their ability to act as bishop. But they themselves had no real desire to become bishop.

Candidate	**Votes Received**
Rev. John G. Innis	377
Rev. J. Sarwolo Nelson, Jr.	308
Rev. Emmanuel F. Bailey	133

Rev. Levi C. Williams	25
Rev. James D. Karblee, Sr.	17
Rev. Anna Kpaan	10
Rev. Herbert Zigbuo	4
Rev. Anthony Dioh	3
Rev. Momo S. Kpaan	3
Rev. Daniel Gueh	2
Rev. Alfred Walker	1
Rev. Samuel Brown	1

Round Two

Rev. John G. Innis	440
Rev. J. Sarwolo Nelson, Jr.	340
Rev. Emmanuel F. Bailey	99
Rev. Levi C. Williams	16
Rev. James D. Karblee	10

Round Three

Rev. Dr. John G. Innis	486
Rev. J. Sarwolo Nelson, Jr.	351
Rev. Emmanuel F. Bailey	74

Nominating Committee for the Gbarnga Conference

Bro. Lawrence A. Morgan, Chairperson
Rev. Alfred S. Walker, Co-chairperson
Sis. Cymbeline D. Bass, Secretary
Mth. Comfort T. Nimineh-Logan
Bro. T. Teah Swen
Sis. Sharon Padmore
Bro. J. Larmark Cox
Rev. James Z. Labala
Rev. Francis Nah Nyemoh
Bro. Mousa A. Dassama, Sr.

Rev. P. Nicol Boyce, I
Bro. George D. Moore
Rev. S. Edward Holt
Rev. Milton K. Freeman
Sis. Nettie Hampton

The Monrovia Election (WACC)

Minutes of the 5th Annual Session of the West Africa Central Conference (WACC), United Methodist Church, Monrovia, Liberia, December 13-17, 2000.

One Voting Round

Candidate	***Votes Received***
Rev. Dr. John G. Innis	39
Rev. J. Sarwolo Nelson, Jr.	19
	2 abstentions
Total Votes	60

Conference Delegations

SIERRA LEONE ANNUAL CONFERENCE—20

Clergy	**Laity**
Rev. J. K. C. Renner	Bro. Max Boiler
Rev. Etta N. Nicol	Bro. F. Carew
Rev. B. T. Tommy	Bro. Eke Halloway
Rev. Sam Kpakra	Sis. S. Harleston
Rev. W. Foonie	Bro. E. Cobba
Rev. J. S. Lomboi	Bro. S. Senesie
Rev. Karimu	Bro. S. A. Koroma
Rev. D. H. Caulker	Sis. Beatrice Fotanah

Rev. M. T. Massaquoi	Sis. Mariam Bah
Rev. Mary Johnson Massaquoi	Bro. J. P. Koroma

NIGERIA ANNUAL CONFERENCE—20

Clergy	**Laity**
Rev. Shammer S. Yugudo	Bro. Laizam Lliya
Rev. James B. Vock	Bro. Napoleron Adnmu
Rev. Ketas K. Mouule	Sis. Mary Y. Jatutu
Rev. Salomatu M. Yaro	Bro. Francis Jommy
Rev. Luka Zanya	Bro. Henry Jusu
Rev. Laitu J. Kone	Bro. Charles H. Yule
Rev. Penu A. John	Bro. Peter Marubiyobo
Rev. Abbo Z. Makili	Sis. LukeBitrus
Rev. Anthony G. Darburannes	Bro. Solomon Olusinnyi
Rev. John Wesley Yahona	Bro. Sunday T. Manyaki

LIBERIA ANNUAL CONFERENCE—20

Clergy	**Laity**
Rev. Emmanuel F. Bailey	Bro. T. Teah Swen
Rev. Robert N. Sieh, Sr.	Bro. George D. Moore
Rev. James D. Karblee, Sr.	Cllr. Musa D. Dassama, Sr.
Rev. S. R. E. Dixon	Bro. J. Lamark Cox, Sr.
Rev. J. Sarwolo Nelson, Jr	Bro. Bobby Wozee
Rev. Anna S. Kpaan	Cllr. Lawrence Morgan
Rev. Momoh S. Kpaan	Bro. Nippy Toe Jackson
Rev. John G. Innis	Sis. Comfort Logan
Rev. Francis Nah Nyemoh	Sis. Agatha R. Bedell
Rev. John S. M. Russell	Sis. Mai Cooper

Officiating Bishops

[The bishops had no voting rights except to break a tie when necessary.]

Rev. Dr. John Hopkins, Presiding Bishop, Representative of the Council of Bishops, UMC
Rev. Dr. Joseph C. Humper, Resident Bishop, Sierra Leone Annual Conference, UMC
Rev. Dr. Done Peter Debala, Resident Bishop, Nigeria Annual Conference, UMC
Rev. Dr. Arthur F. Kulah, Resident Bishop, Liberia Annual Conference, UMC